SAVORING MEXICO

Books by Sharon Cadwallader

WHOLE EARTH COOK BOOK
IN CELEBRATION OF SMALL THINGS
COOKING ADVENTURES FOR KIDS
WHOLE EARTH COOK BOOK 2
SHARON CADWALLADER'S COMPLETE COOKBOOK
SHARING IN THE KITCHEN
SAVORING MEXICO

SAVORING MEXICO

*Classic Recipes of Traditional Cuisine
from All Regions of Mexico*

Sharon Cadwallader

Chronicle Books

First Chronicle Books Edition 1987

Printed in the United States of America.

Library of Congress Cataloging in Publication Data
Cadwallader, Sharon.
Savoring Mexico.
Includes index.
1. Cookery, Mexican. 2. Mexico—Description and
travel, 1951—
I. Title
TX716.M4C32   641.5972   80-36772
ISBN: 0-87701-427-2

The author is grateful to Indiana University Press,
which gave permission to quote from the poetry
of Ramón López Velarde: from *Anthology of
Mexican Poetry* by Octavio Paz, translated
by Samuel Beckett; copyright © 1958 by Indiana
University Press.

Cover design: Thomas Ingalls and Associates
Cover photograph: Joel Glenn
Food Stylist: Cherie Miller
Book design: Anita Walker Scott
Illustrations: Gary Wulfsberg
Maps: Linda Griggs

Chronicle Books
One Hallidie Plaza
San Francisco, CA 94102

FOR MAX *who first showed Mexico to me*

CONTENTS

When the last weariness
comes upon me
I will go to my village
to kneel among
the roses in the square,
the hoops of children
and the silken fringes of shawls.

Ramón López Velarde (1888–1921)

SAVORING MEXICO

INTRODUCTION

*I*ONCE SHOWED a drawing of Mexico to a woman who was the curator of a small museum in California. It had been a gift to me and I valued it because it was the hills of Jalisco, an area that I love. "It's such a beautiful country," she sighed, "and so full of contrasts."

She was right. It is a land of contrasts—sometimes conflicting and confusing, but always compelling. But it's also a land of blends—exciting and curious combinations.

The major contrasts in Mexico now are a result of technological and economic advances. It's a country that seems to move ahead by skipping a step or two of development, omitting links that are important to our sense of progress and order. A modern cement factory, fueled by natural gas, shadows one-room shacks of wood or adobe where the cooking for ten people is done on a charcoal brazier; a sleek and expensive automobile is parked beside a braying donkey pulling a hand-hewn cart; a shopping basket that contains a stack of fresh, hot, handmade tortillas wrapped in brown paper also contains a can of Campbell's Chicken Noodle Soup; a businessman in a three-piece suit and dark glasses leans against the sidewalk juice stand, drinking his morning Vitamin C, oblivious to the somber Indian woman next to him dressed in dark clothing and nursing a baby wrapped in her *rebozo* while she consumes a bottled Coca Cola; high-spirited youths, dressed as modern teen-agers, pave the urban streets with laughter without so much as a glance at the vendor in *huaraches* and a *sombrero* sitting on the sidewalk selling steaming tamales from a single pot in front of him. These contrasts are accepted in Mexico, and are similar to the juxtapositions found in underdeveloped countries everywhere. Yet these differences have a deeper origin, from which come the blends that charm and intrigue the outsider.

1

Mexico has an indomitable geography, with over two-thirds of its land either hilly or mountainous. The great ranges, the Sierra Madre Occidental and the Sierra Madre Oriental, are like two long arms thrown to the sea, only to succeed in cutting off the coastal valleys from the interior and creating radical changes in temperature, and difficulties in farming and transportation. The center of the country, from Colima to Orizaba, is marked by a line of volcanoes created from a series of earthquakes, and the surrounding terrain, rugged and torn by the upheavals, is fraught with drainage problems. In addition, a large part of Mexico lies in a latitude where rainfall is variable and in sharp contradiction from north to south. For a nation dependent on agriculture, especially on the soil-ravaging corn crop, these climatic and topographical conditions have had enormous effects on economic stability.

Mexico's history has also been influenced by contrasts. A country of separate and combined Spanish and Indian blood, it contains the features of both of these old civilizations along with a culture of its own. Curiously, the strengths of both the Indian and the Spaniard have prevailed—perhaps more than in any other Latin American country. Politics, folk art, architecture, religion, music, literature, family structure, personal honor, all represent the two heritages. Although the official language of Mexico is Spanish, it is not the Castilian Spanish spoken in Spain, but has an intonation and accent of its own. (Some say there is no better Spanish than that of the well-spoken Mexican.) In addition, many Indian dialects are still spoken in Mexico.

It is this dual theme of contrasting and blending that has given shape to Mexican cuisine. To me, Mexico is a symphony of food smells. Just as it is possible to pick out the dominant instrument in a musical piece, you can identify the pungency of fresh *cilantro* and *chiles* in a Mexican market. But the background odors, like the supportive sections of an orchestra, create the overall effect.

The Americas are rich in indigenous foods that dominate Mexican cuisine. Corn was the staple of all the Indians in the Americas and dates back to the beginning of their civilizations. Peppers, too, in all their sweet and fiery forms, are American.

They have been pollinated by the wind and are profuse and varied, partly due to the differences in soil and rainfall. Potatoes, beans, squash, avocados, tomatoes (both red and the husked green variety) were early Indian crops. Peanuts were cultivated in Latin America about the same time as they were grown in Africa. And the luxuries, vanilla and chocolate, were both brought back to Europe from Mexico by the conquistadors.

Conversely, the Spaniards brought to Mexico (and to the Americas in general) foods from their kitchens, although many of the items had their origin in the Mediterranean and in Asia and were the result of the Moorish influence in Spain. Rice, nuts, citrus fruits, coriander (*cilantro*), cattle, pigs, chickens, capers, saffron, and a variety of herbs and spices were brought in by the Spanish. During the brief French rule in the mid-nineteenth century European cheeses were introduced into the country, and small commercial bakeries emerged. Now, French rolls (*bolillos* in Mexico) and delicate pastries are a fundamental part of the Mexican diet.

Mexico, like every country, has its special, regional dishes. But nowadays, advances in communication and transportation have moved ingredients about so easily that it is possible, for example, to find an authentic Yucatecan dish on the west coast or in the northeastern part of the country. While this book is divided into various geographical sections of Mexico, they are not strictly regional in terms of cuisine. The book itself is a product of one long journey throughout the country, added on to a number of earlier shorter trips and extended stays. On these travels I have collected recipes for dishes that appealed to me even if they were not traditional in their particular areas. The recipes I have included in this book are those that I feel are most representative of Mexican cuisine in general and easy to prepare outside of Mexico. However, there are still some ingredients that are not readily available in some parts of the United States and Canada. Whenever possible, I have made adjustments and substitutions for ingredients, and have altered the directions to make the recipes more accessible to the reader (e.g., while there are many *chiles,* fresh and dried, north of the Mexican border, not all varieties common to Mexico can be found, so I have substituted those that I think work well). Under the circumstances, and knowing the Mexican sense of resourcefulness, I felt an occasional wink at tradition would be acceptable. *BUEN PROVECHO!*

SHARON CADWALLADER

CHAPTER ONE

The Northeast

MONTERREY

WHENEVER I cross into Mexico I feel an immediate shift in atmosphere. It's not necessarily the topography, especially coming from West Texas where the spare landscape differs little from the desolate plains of northern Mexico. It may be the smells, or the air on my skin, but as soon as I move a few yards south of the border I know I'm in another country—unmistakable Mexico!

Of course, this is quickly verified, not only by the language, but on first contact with any Mexican border official. Mexicans seem to love paperwork. Customs people spend a staggering amount of time (yours, since you are the one who is anxious to get going) filling out documents in triplicate on old, manual typewriters, with worn carbon paper. Every copy is notarized resoundingly and you are then sent on to another desk or office for a repeat performance. It can provoke some impatience in the foreigner, especially if it is a hot day. However, the wait always ends on a convivial note with the car inspector (the final official) shaking the driver's hand wherein a few pesos are waiting. Then he wishes you a *buen viaje* as you begin your journey down into the country.

On the last two trips to Mexico, we (my brother Gary and I) entered the Ciudad Acuna in the state of Coahuila. Crossing here seems to be less hectic than at Juárez or Nuevo Laredo, and the highways from the border are in much the same condition. Mexico will never be known for its smooth roadwork, one very good reason not to travel by automobile at night. Maybe the highway department has a small budget for repairs or perhaps it's the abundance of manual laborers that makes them rely on simple tools and techniques. Workmen leave the job at the end of the day with only a couple of white-painted stones (if that) in the road to warn the night driver of a 3 × 5-foot ditch in his or her path.

But I should also give credit to Mexican roadbuilding. The country is astoundingly rugged and uneven to conquer for transportation. That they have managed to connect it so well (e.g., the highway from Mexico City to Oaxaca) is a phenomena of engineering and an indication of their competence and perseverance. These two traits may also account for their luck on the road. As fearless and fast as Mexicans are behind the wheel, the accident rate is remarkably low. On this last trip, zig-zagging over 10,000 miles around the country, we saw only one accident. A new van with New York plates had turned over on the road from Mérida to Campeche.

Driving south to Saltillo, the capital of Coahuila, we passed through a number of small settlements, the final affirmation of arriving in Mexico. In no way does Zaragoza, the first town of any size, resemble a west Texas town. Further on, about 150 miles south of the border is Monclova, the approximate location of Padre Miguel Hidalgo's "Waterloo." In February 1811, an ex-rebel commander ambushed the remaining revolutionary army on their trek north into what is now Texas, where they were planning to regroup and rearm. It was a sad day in the history of Mexican independence but there is little reference to it in Monclova, just another busy northern Mexican city.

Saltillo claims over 200,000 *habitantes,* but it seems smaller. The old, low adobe buildings that blend with the landscape make it look like a movie set of a Texas-Mexican town. Settled over two hundred years ago, Saltillo was the capital when this large northeastern territory included Texas. A few miles outside of the city is the Augosturo/Buenavista Battlefield where General Zachary Taylor defeated General Santa Anna in the Mexican-American War of 1846–48. Actually the victory in February 1847 was pyrrhic—Santa Anna crept away during the night to mourn his losses, and Taylor, not certain of his next move, hung on and proclaimed victory, thus halting the upward Mexican thrust until a peace treaty was signed the following year. So ignominious is this battle in Mexican history that it is remembered only by a small, almost undetectable, monument out on the battlegrounds.

Saltillo is better known for its blankets and its beef. Beautiful,

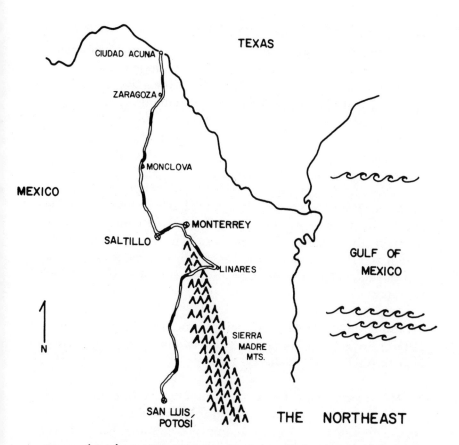

TEXAS

CIUDAD ACUÑA

ZARAGOZA

MONCLOVA

MEXICO

MONTERREY

SALTILLO

LINARES

GULF OF
MEXICO

SIERRA
MADRE
MTS.

N

SAN LUIS,
POTOSI

THE NORTHEAST

warm-colored *sarapes* are woven and sold in the markets and
shops. The local restaurants feature many delicious meat dishes.
One of my favorites is *Empanadas de Picadillo* (Savory Meat
Turnovers). *Empanadas* are popular all over Mexico and I have
had them stuffed with fish, chicken, and pork. There are also
sweet *Empanadas* filled with fruit or jam.

EMPANADAS DE PICADILLO

(Savory Meat Turnovers)
PASTRY:

3 cups all-purpose flour	½ cup lard
1½ teaspoons baking powder	Ice water (½ to ⅔ cup)
¾ teaspoon salt	Lard or oil for frying

FILLING:

1 medium onion, minced

⅓ cup oil

2 cups shredded boiled beef (*Carne Deshebrada,* page 16)

1 large potato, cooked, peeled, and diced

½ cup raisins, chopped

⅛ teaspoon each cinnamon, cloves, and cumin

Salt

½ cup medium-dry cooking sherry

TO MAKE PASTRY: Sift together flour, baking powder, and salt, and cut in lard to a crumbly consistency. Add enough ice water to make the dough stick together. (The less you work this dough and the less water you use, the lighter the crust.) Thinly roll out dough on a floured board and cut into 3½- to 4-inch rounds.

TO PREPARE FILLING: Sauté onion in oil until limp. Add meat, potato, raisins, seasonings, and salt to taste. Stir and cook to heat through. Pour in sherry.

TO MAKE *empanadas:* Put a small amount of filling on one side of each circle, (enough so you can fold over the other half and seal.) Dip fork in cold water and press edges together with fork tines. Let sit for 30 minutes on one side and then turn and let sit for another 30 minutes—this helps to dry and seal the edges. Fry in about ¼ inch of hot oil or lard until golden brown on each side. Serve hot or cold, with lime if desired. Makes about 20 *empanadas.*

North central Mexico is meat country. Chihuahua has always been known as the major cattle state, and the entire state (the largest in Mexico) was once owned by only a few families who maintained some of the largest ranches in the world. The expertise in meat cooking extends as far west as Sonora and east to Monterrey. Here in Saltillo we discovered another dish worth mentioning, *Topada de Lengua* (Smothered Tongue). Slices of tongue are served in a rich wine and caper sauce in small earthen casseroles. Tongue, incidentally, is used in this area in tacos and burritos as commonly as shredded beef or pork.

TOPADA DE LENGUA
(Smothered Tongue)

1 small beef tongue (2 to 2½ pounds	4 teaspoons capers
1 medium onion, thinly sliced	1 medium tomato, peeled and chopped
1 *chile jalapeño* seeded and sliced	⅔ cup rich beef broth
2 tablespoons oil	¼ teaspoon salt
1 tablespoon butter	⅛ teaspoon cinnamon
3 cloves garlic, minced	Pinch cloves
	¼ cup dry sherry

Prepare tongue as directed on page 16. Peel and trim but do not shred. Slice in ⅛-inch pieces. Place pieces at the bottom of a large frying pan. In another frying pan, sauté onion and chile slices in oil and butter until well softened but not browned. Add garlic and continue to sauté. Stir in capers, tomatoes, broth, and seasonings and cover pan. Simmer for 10 to 12 minutes or until tomato is well blended. Add sherry and pour all ingredients over tongue slices. Cover pan and simmer all ingredients for 5 minutes. Serve in 4 small casseroles or ramekins with *Arroz a la Mexicana*, page 22. Serves 4.

The climate of Saltillo is generally pleasant—sunny and dry. It is almost a mile high in spite of its low-lying feeling. On a previous trip through Saltillo on our way to San Luis Potosí we were turned back because of snow and ice on the highway. It had been cold in Saltillo when we arrived the night before, and in the morning the hotel gardens were covered with snow. It was a real surprise to us, but apparently snow is not uncommon. We detoured over to Monterrey, only fifty miles away, but

3,500 feet lower. Then we traveled south along Highway 85 just far enough so that we could cross back to the Constitutional Highway without fear of ice.

On this most recent trip to Mexico, we spent more time in Monterrey to get a better feel for it. Actually, I don't think I feel any better about it, but it is more familiar. Monterrey is now the second largest city in Mexico, very industrial and active, with a wild traffic situation. Most small towns in Mexico are laid out in a grid, but planning in larger cities is different. It's true that many settlements lie in the crevices of this furrowed country and understandably curve and wind—like the colonial city of Guanajuato which snakes through a narrow ravine. But these cities, difficult to negotiate at best, are even more inaccessible to the foreigner because of the seemingly disorganized traffic flow. I mention this advisedly, because it just may be that I have never been able to figure out the traffic plans or laws. Then again, there may be none. Anyway, city traffic is chilling to the newcomer. And it's further compounded by all the *glorietas,* or traffic circles, that dot the main streets of the cities. These circles serve nicely as bases for statues of war heroes or presidents, but the traffic patterns around them seem indiscernible. Every driver maneuvers independently of the next.

I don't mean to belabor Mexican transit here, but it's quite the topic of conversation for tourists. If driving at night is ill-advised, so is driving in cities. Fortunately there is an abundance of inexpensive public transportation. And it's walking country, anyway.

Monterrey is the goat meat capital and is very barbecue-oriented. There are several restaurants that feature barbecued kid, although I think the best I ever tasted was in a charming patio restaurant in León, Guanajuato. Needless to say, I am not including a recipe for barbecued goat, or for any goat dish, as it is not a common meat in most of North America.

We ate one night at the well-known *Regio* restaurant in Monterrey, a large open-air patio with raging, wood barbecues. We had beef ribs, which, while tasty, were also tough as Mexican beef can be. They were served nicely on a small hibachi to keep the meat warm, and with accompanying bowls of chopped, fresh cilantro, chopped onions, and an excellent *Salsa Cruda* (Uncooked Tomato Sauce).

A word about Mexican sauces: the sauce is the added flavor (and often fire) in Mexican food. Sauces were a part of the Indian kitchen, and also a part of the Spanish cuisine. In the past, there was hardly a restaurant in the country, however modest, that did not have a bowl of freshly made tomato sauce on every table. However, I did notice some change on my last trip through the country. It seems that the food industry has crept in, even to the mom-and-pop restaurants. And instead of a homemade sauce I often found several bottles of commercial hot sauce on the table. But if I asked for *la salsa de la casa* (the house sauce) I was usually brought a bowl of a good, fresh tomato sauce of their own. These sauces vary throughout the republic. Sometimes the tomatoes are cooked. Usually they contain onion and chiles (hot or mild), sometimes garlic and/or cilantro, lime, oregano, and salt and they are eaten with meat, fish, chicken, vegetables, eggs, beans, plain tortillas, etc.

SALSA CRUDA
(Uncooked Tomato Sauce)

2 small tomatoes, unpeeled	1 to 2 fresh *chiles serranos* or 1 fresh *chile jalapeño*
½ medium onion, chopped	¼ cup chopped cilantro
	2 tablespoons cold water
	Salt to taste

Chop tomatoes and mix with chopped onions and chiles that have not been seeded. Add cilantro, water, and salt to taste. Makes about 1½ to 1¾ cups.

We had wonderful *Nachos con Queso* (Fried Tortilla Chips with Cheese) at the Regio. It is my hunch that *nachos* prepared like this originated in northern Mexico where there is good rich milk cheese for broiling. The most successful equivalent to *queso asadero* (broiling cheese) available in the United States is Muenster. Monterey Jack can also be used.

NACHOS CON QUESO
(Fried Tortilla Chips with Cheese)

1 dozen stale corn tortillas
Corn oil for frying
Salt
Grated or sliced Muenster
or Monterey Jack cheese

5 canned pickled (*en escabeche*) *chiles jalapeños*, stemmed and sliced
Lime wedges

Leave tortillas out of the package for several hours in the sun or overnight and they will be stale enough. Tear each tortilla into 8 pieces. Pour ¼ inch oil in heavy-bottomed frying pan or pot and heat oil to 350°. Fry tortilla pieces 2 to 3 minutes and salt lightly. Chips should be crisp but chewy, too. Add more oil if necessary. Drain on paper towels. Spread chips on baking sheet very close together and sprinkle or lay over cheese. Distribute chile pieces over cheese and broil until cheese melts together. Serve immediately with lime wedges.

Another well-known dish discovered in this area is *Machaca de Monterrey* which uses dried beef. Making dried beef or jerky was one way the northern plains people could preserve their big slaughters for use in future months. For this recipe, the jerky is pounded and shredded, fried with tomatoes, onions, and chiles, and then scrambled with eggs as a filling for flour tortillas. You can also make this recipe with *Carne Deshebrada* (Shredded Boiled Beef).

MACHACA DE MONTERREY
(Shredded Beef with Eggs)

3 small tomatoes,
   unpeeled
1 small onion
3 *chiles serranos*
½ cup oil
2½ cups shredded beef

(see *Carne Seca* page
15, or *Carne
Deshebrada* page 16)
2 teaspoons lime juice
6 eggs, lightly beaten
Flour tortillas

Chop tomatoes and onion. Chop chiles finely and mix all together. Heat oil in heavy-bottomed frying pan and fry ingredients for 6 to 8 minutes until they become sauce-like. Add beef and lime juice and cook a few minutes more. Add lightly beaten eggs and cook and stir until set. Serve as a filling for warm, flour tortillas. Serve with lime and *Salsa Cruda* (page 13) if desired. Serves 4 to 5.

CARNE SECA
(Dried Meat)

2 pounds beef rump
4 large limes

2 teaspoons oregano
Salt

Slice beef very thin across the grain and trim off gristle or fat. Lay pieces on shallow baking trays without touching. Squeeze limes and mix juice with oregano. Sprinkle or brush meat with lime marinade and salt lightly. Cover and refrigerate overnight. In the morning place in a low (200°) oven for 6 hours or until meat is hard and dry all the way through. Store in a covered plastic container. Eat as jerky or pound and shred for taco filling or for use in the following recipe.

CARNE DESHEBRADA
(Shredded Boiled Beef)

2 pounds beef rump, tongue, or 2½ pounds chuck	Water
1 small onion, sliced	Salt
3 cloves garlic, minced	Bay leaf
	Juice of 2 limes

Trim beef of bone, fat, and gristle and cut into 3- to 4-inch pieces. (Scrub whole tongue but trim after cooking.) Place in a saucepan with onion and garlic and cover with water. Salt amply and add bay leaf. Bring to a boil, reduce heat and simmer until meat is tender. Drain (save broth for soups or other recipes) and shred meat while still warm. Store in covered container for making *machaca* (page 15) or *empanadas* (page 9.)

Leaving Monterrey south on Highway 85 is a long process. The town stretches out, rather prettily at times, and there are a number of lovely residential areas on the outskirts. We also passed the well-known *Monterrey Instituto de Technológico*, the MIT of Mexico, founded by one of the major industrial families of Monterrey.

Mexican highways leading in and out of cities are often built up above the surrounding land. This is partly for drainage (especially important in the tropics where the rains are often sudden and violent), and also because it is safer for the travelers, carts, and animals that use the paths on either side of the road.

As we get closer to the Gulf of Mexico there appears an entirely different landscape. Radical climatic and topographical changes are some of the remarkable features of Mexico. The area around Monterrey is barren compared to southern Nuevo León which is fairly tropical with lush foliage, bright flowers, and miles of orange groves on either side of the highway. Orange trees are a common sight in the warm coastal states of Mexico, and there are many roadside stands selling wonderful, greenish, juice oranges for practically nothing. Such stands sell fresh juice also, one of my favorite treats in Mexico and reminiscent of the orange juice stands of the early 1940s in southern California. In fact, there are juice stands everywhere in Mexico—in the open markets, along the streets, and beside historical and archaeological monuments. Even venders with primitive hand-wheeled carts sell juice in front of the most modern city buildings or plush residences.

Mexico is unconsciously health food country. People everywhere buy fresh fruit and vegetable juices. (The electric blender is the greatest gift since the tortilla machine.) Of course, they drink a lot of soda pop, too. It is said that once the children of Mexico had very white, strong teeth, a result of the lime in the processing of corn for tortillas. But the heavy soda pop consumption of the last two decades is changing the statistics.

Linares is a bustling town, just a few miles north of the Nuevo León-Tamaulipas border. It is here that one can turn west and cut through the Sierra Madre Oriental Mountains to meet the Constitutional Highway to San Luis Potosí.

On this last trip we stopped for a breather in Linares where I had one of the best chicken soups I have tasted in Mexico. *Sopa de Pollo* or *Consomé de Pollo* are the most common soups in Mexico. Although the ingredients vary from region to region, the broth is predictably good. Mexico seems to raise flavorful chickens, maybe because they are allowed to scratch naturally or perhaps because the meat is often tough and is therefore cooked a long time at a low heat. At any rate, it is a good, safe food order wherever you are in the country.

The chicken soup was accompanied by a basket of fresh, hot *bolillos,* the famous French roll of Mexico. The Spanish brought wheat flour breads to Mexico, and during the brief occupation of the French more breads and pastries were introduced into the country. There is no village of any consequence that does not have a small *Panadería* (bakery) where delicious breads and pastries are baked daily. Batches of *bolillos* are often baked several times in one day. My favorite Mexican cookie is a spongecake roll, dripping with rum, and wrapped individually.

These were prepared several times a week in one of the bakeries in the city of Guanajuato. I did not find them on my last visit although I heard they were still being made. Unfortunately, I did not get the recipe on my previous visit.

SOPA DE POLLO
(Chicken Soup)

This was served with a little portion of pickled chile jalapeños and lots of lime wedges.

1 large chicken with giblets (preferably a fat stewing hen)
1 large carrot, sliced
1 medium onion, quartered
2 cloves garlic
Salt and pepper

Water
1 handful of rice
2 medium carrots, thinly sliced
2 small zucchini, diced
1 cup fresh or frozen peas
Salt and pepper

In a large pot put disjointed chicken and giblets. Add carrot, onion, garlic, and salt and pepper amply. Cover with cold water and simmer, covered, for several hours—until chicken is very tender and falls from bone. Strain off broth and cool. Remove and discard chicken skin and bones saving chicken meat. Refrigerate broth and skim off fat. Return broth and chicken to pot and add rice. Simmer for 15 minutes and add carrots. Simmer for another 15 minutes and add zucchini and peas. Simmer 10 minutes. Season to taste and serve. Serves 4 to 6.

BOLILLOS
(French Rolls)

2 cups lukewarm water
1 package dry yeast
2 teaspoons salt
¼ cup sugar

5 cups unbleached flour (hard wheat is best)
1 tablespoon cornstarch
⅓ cup cold water

Stir together water, yeast, salt, and sugar. Beat in (using electric or hand beater) 2 cups of flour, then stir in 2½ cups more to make a sticky, but firm dough. Flour board with remaining ½ cup flour and turn out dough. Knead for 5 to 6 minutes only and then transfer dough to an oiled bowl. Let rise (covered) in a warm place until doubled in bulk (about 1½ hours). Punch down dough and divide into 12 equal pieces. Roll each piece into a ball between your palms and then pull the ends into a long roll shape. Place on a greased baking sheet and, with a sharp knife that has been dipped in cold water, make a lengthwise slash in the top of each roll—½ inch from each end and about ½ inch deep. Brush tops of rolls with cornstarch mixed with water and put rolls in preheated 450° oven. Place a long baking pan of boiling water on the rack below the rolls to make a nice crusty exterior. After 10 minutes reduce heat to 375° and bake until rolls are golden brown (about 20 minutes). Serve warm or reheat before serving. Makes 1 dozen.

The western detour from Linares is fascinating. We took this road after the snow in Saltillo forced us to change our route, and again on this last trip, finding the terrain different and unpredictable each time. After reaching a plateau in the climb, the landscape changed from the densely wooded foothills of madrone and scrub oak to mountains and evergreens. We emerged on a gigantic plateau, 7,000 or 8,000 feet high, with a strange Siberian-like landscape of rugged *barrancas* and Joshua trees that looked like armies of supernatural creatures. On the first trip, we found patches of snow and it was incredibly windy and cold, but on the last ride it was warmer. The scarcity of growth made me also think of African plains and I half expected to see antelope and giraffe bounding by the car windows. Back on the Constitutional Highway the road is straight and rather tedious to San Luis Potosí. The only curiosity was the children who held up their hands that clutched little live birds or lizards—anything to sell in order to survive that stubborn dry soil.

San Luis Potosí is a growing city. I had been to Mexico many times before I had an opportunity to visit it, although I had heard much about the city from a Mexican friend whose father ran the Ford agency there. From his descriptions, and because he was an architect of the contemporary Mexican school, I imagined it to be industrial and hard-edged. It is quite a city for commerce, and one of the major connecting arteries in the highway and railway systems of Mexico. There are many factories and businesses on the city outskirts. Much of this activity comes from the fact that the area was once a mining center, when silver and gold were extracted from the nearby San Pedro hills. San Luis Potosí, like the city of Zacatecas, was founded to accommodate the ore-related activities and it is still a significant processing center, with one of the largest smelters in the country.

But San Luis Potosí was more than I expected. Heavily settled by missionaries anxious to glean some of the mining wealth for the church, the city has a definite colonial flavor toward its center. Elaborate civic buildings, churches and residences grace narrow streets laced by trees and flowering shrubbery. The city is named after the great mines of Potosí, Bolivia, and in the early days was expected to become one of the most wealthy and cultural cities of Mexico.

San Luis Potosí also figures heavily in Mexico's political history. It was the headquarters of the ruthless General Calleja who hunted and defeated Hidalgo on the banks of the Lerma River near Guadalajara. It functioned as a temporary capital for Benito Juárez in his struggle to end French intervention in Mexico. And most recently, San Luis Potosí was the namesake for Francisco Madero's *Plan de Luis*. The intense but sincere Madero, imprisoned by President Porfirio Díaz in San Luis Potosí, drew up a plan that called for a general uprising against Díaz. The spark was kindled, and within a year, thirty-five years of dictatorship had ended in Mexico.

San Luis Potosí lacks no less fascination in crafts and cuisine. The lovely, tiled mall, *Calle Hidalgo*, is full of shops selling a variety of Mexico's finest wares. The most beautiful to me were elegant silk shawls made in the nearby village of Santa María del

Río. Sold in the marketplace nearby is one of the regional food specialties, *queso de tuna* (literally "tuna cheese"), a sweet paste made from the fruit of the *nopal* cactus. In the United States we call this cactus "prickly pear" and in Mexico the fruit is called *fruta de tuna*. I didn't bother to find out about the preparation of this paste because, although chopped *nopales* (the paddles of the cactus) are found in Mexican markets in the Southwest, I had never seen the fruit sold in this country. However *nopal* cactus *does* grow in the United States and recently I discovered a great field of it less than an hour's drive from my home.

Wandering around San Luis Potosí we came across a compact little restaurant with a wonderful aroma. Here we tried a delicious *sopa de cebolla* (onion soup). It was remarkably French-like, except that it contained a bit of cream.

SOPA DE CEBOLLO CON CREMA
(Onion Soup with Cream)

5 medium onions, thinly sliced	1 cup heavy cream or Mexican *crema* (page 119)
2 tablespoons sweet butter	Salt, nutmeg
2 tablespoons corn oil	Muenster or Monterey Jack cheese, grated
4 tablespoons flour	Lime wedges
1½ quarts rich chicken broth	

In a heavy soup pot, sauté onions in combined butter and oil until golden (18 to 20 minutes). Sprinkle flour over top and stir while adding broth. Cover and simmer for ½ hour and add cream slowly so it will not curdle. Heat through and season to taste. Pour in individual, shallow bowls and top amply with grated cheese. Place bowls under a broiler until cheese is well melted. Serve immediately with lime wedges. Serves 5 to 6.

One evening we crossed the city to visit *La Virreina* restaurant on Carranza Boulevard. This was an elegant experience as the restaurant is in an old colonial mansion that was built in the early nineteenth century. The house had obviously been opened up for dining, but it still retained the stately high-ceilinged style of the colonial period. There is a long entrance hall that opens into a two-level dining area. We sat under a portrait, pristinely stylized in the early Spanish tradition. A young girl carrying a small caged bird, and standing by a shrine of the Virgin, is flanked by two other woeful-eyed maidens. It's a little difficult to tell exactly what is going on, but it's a touching scene.

We ordered *Puntas de Filete* (Sirloin Tips) that were served in a savory sauce of simple ingredients, and the waiter was only too willing to tell me how it was prepared. Mexican waiters all seem to know how to cook, or at least are very observant in the kitchen. The meat was served on a long platter with *Arroz a la Mexicana* (Mexican Rice), and we augmented all this with ice cold Bohemia beer served in tall wine glasses. On the way out of the restaurant my brother said *nos vemos,* to mean a leisurely, "we'll see you." The waiter smiled in an amused fashion. Gary shrugged, "That must not be a Potosían idiom."

ARROZ A LA MEXICANA
(Mexican Rice)

2 cups long-grain rice	⅓ cup light oil
Hot water	Salt
1 large tomato, peeled and seeded	4 cups chicken broth or half broth and half water
½ medium onion, quartered	½ cup peas
2 cloves garlic	Avocado slices

Cover rice with hot water and let sit to swell for about 15 minutes, then drain off water. Rinse several times with cold water until water runs clear of the starch. Drain well and set rice aside. Put tomato, onion, and garlic in blender and purée.

Heat oil in heavy-bottomed pan and stir in rice to coat grains. Fry rice until golden over a high heat, stirring all the while. Add purée and continue to fry and stir until rice is quite dry. Salt lightly and pour broth or broth combination over mixture. Stir once and then lower heat to simmer. Cover and continue to cook for about 20 minutes, without stirring until broth is absorbed. Let sit for 10 minutes or so, then stir in hot, cooked peas and serve garnished with avocado slices. Serves 5 to 6.

PUNTAS DE FILETE EN SALSA MEXICANA
(Sirloin Tips in Mexican Sauce)

4 tablespoons olive oil	1 cup rich chicken broth
2 pounds beef sirloin, cut in 1-inch pieces	3 tablespoons minced parsley
Salt	2 sprigs fresh oregano
3 tablespoons sweet butter	3 *chiles serranos,* seeded and minced
½ cup minced onion	3 tablespoons sherry
3 cloves garlic, mashed	
5 cups tomatoes, peeled, seeded and chopped	

Heat oil in heavy-bottomed skillet and add meat. Brown meat lightly over a medium heat and salt lightly. Add butter, onion, and garlic and sauté until onions are limp. Add tomatoes, broth, parsley, oregano, and chiles. Cover and simmer over a low heat for 10 minutes. Remove cover, increase heat to medium-high and reduce sauce until it is thick and well blended. Add salt to taste and sherry. Serve with *Arroz a la Mexicana.* Serves 5.

CHAPTER TWO

The East Coast

VERACRUZ

I HAD wanted to see Tampico since I first heard the Andrews Sisters sing their immortal mispronunciation of the city's name. (The accent is on the second syllable.) It's a catchy tune, though, and I knew the city would be well worth the visit. Early one morning we started the misty, winding descent from the Sierra Madre Mountains out onto the flat, green, coastal plain.

We stopped in a pleasant little town, Río Verde, to make *tortas* for lunch (this translates to something like hotcake, but colloquially it refers to a sandwich made with a French roll or *bolillo.*) We bought the hot, fresh rolls from a bakery near the central market, and then stopped at a delicatessen-like store to buy a few thin slices of ham for the filling. Most Mexican towns have these small shops (and now sections in their *supermercados*) where cold meats, cheeses, and dairy products are sold. Ham or bacon sandwiches in Mexico are a wonderful treat because pork, in general, is excellent. *Tortas de jámon* are my favorite lunch on the road, and for making them I always carry a jar of Dijon mustard in the car's glove compartment.

After Río Verde, it was a long journey through the marshy flatlands to get to Tampico proper. As in many other tropical cities and towns in Mexico, the edges are poor and primitive, with a large *barrio* section struggling to stay above the waterline of the constant rains.

Because of a storm, it was overcast in the coastal region. Veracruz, we were to find, had been hard hit and was without electricity for three days. Even though it was December, the air was heavy and damp, and only tolerable because of a slight breeze. I made a mental note never to visit Tampico in the summer. I could imagine how muggy and buggy it must be from May to September. In fact, there's not a lot to be said for

27

the climate along the eastern coastal strip. The wet winds from the Gulf drench the area without mercy and the precipitation is even greater as one travels further south. (On the northern side of the Isthmus of Tehuantepec the rainfall is measured in feet.) Furthermore, the hurricanes circling in from the Caribbean dump wild rain on the eastern foothills, swelling the rivers, causing floods and turning much of the coastal belt into a soggy marsh. Then as an unwelcome reprieve, the *nortes,* cold northern winds, begin to blow in November, sometimes lasting several days.

Tampico lies on the enormous Pánuco River, and before entering the city one passes many run-off ponds and lagoons. To travel south on Highway 180 it is necessary to cross the river by ferry. This ferry runs back and forth all day long, but often there will be a long line of vehicles waiting to cross.

The city grew out of an old Huasteca Indian town, but did not see any great growth until oil was discovered in 1911. Tampico has always felt the effects of its isolation and in its early days was constantly harassed by pirates. Even in this century it has been plagued by highwaymen stalking the payroll to the oilfields. Eventually, it became common practice to fly in the money from Tuxpan.

For all its drawbacks, Tampico is a charming tropical city with narrow streets and high curbs and sidewalks for avoiding the rainwater. Old mansions painted in sherbet colors are crumbling in the dampness, although the grilled gates and windows give the effect of an overall elegance. Evenings in tropical towns are long and active. Stores and restaurants stay open late, sidewalks are crowded, and the air is noisy with traffic and music. It's a good city for the stroller.

Tampico offers much for adventure and recreation. In fact, it is a big sports area with guides and boats available for hunting, river fishing, and deep-sea angling. Ten miles east of the city is the beach, Playa Miramar, with modestly priced beach-front hotels and a clean, warm surf for bathing.

Tampico's best feature for me was the shrimp. It is one of the major seafood centers in Mexico, and the Gulf supports the largest shrimp industry in the world (but how they will

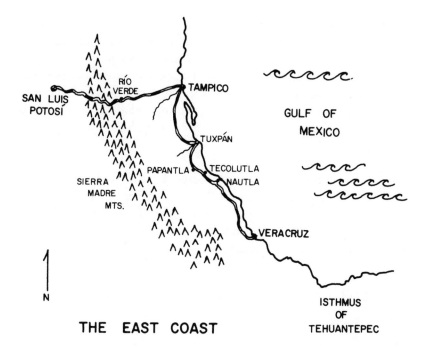

survive future oil spills remains to be seen). We ate wonderful *Camarones a la Plancha* (Grilled Shrimp) more than once. There may be no better culinary combination than grilled shrimp, *Arroz a la Mexicana* (Mexican Rice, page 22), and cold Mexican beer, especially in Tampico, the home of *Negra Modelo,* the dark Corona beer.

CAMARONES A LA PLANCHA

(Grilled Shrimp)

2 pounds large fresh shrimp	1 scant teaspoon salt
⅓ cup unsalted butter, melted	¼ teaspoon hot, red-pepper sauce
⅓ cup olive oil	2 tablespoons minced parsley
¼ cup lime juice	

Wash shrimp and dry well. Mix together all other ingredients in a bowl and add shrimp. Coat shrimp well with marinade and let sit at room temperature (but not in too warm of a spot) for 35 to 40 minutes, turning several times. Arrange on skewers and grill 3 inches from a hot fire for 3 to 5 minutes on each side (depending on size of shrimp). Serve immediately with *Arroz a la Mexicana* (page 22) and lime wedges. Serves 5 to 6.

Another remarkable shrimp recipe I found in Tampico was the *Tortilla de Camarones y Espinaca* (Shrimp and Spinach Omelet). On the table was a wonderful *Salsa Perejil* (Parsley Sauce), as versatile as any house sauce, but an especially good running-mate with the omelet.

TORTILLA DE CAMARONES Y ESPINACA
(Shrimp and Spinach Omelet)

½ cup finely-chopped scallions
⅔ cup finely-chopped red pepper
2 tablespoons chopped *chile serrano* (optional)
3 tablespoons olive oil
3 cups finely-chopped fresh spinach

1 teaspoon each oregano and salt
½ pound tiny fresh shrimp, poached
8 eggs
3 tablespoons cold water

Sauté scallions, peppers, and chile in hot oil in a large (10½-inch frying pan) until softened. Add spinach and seasonings and continue to sauté until spinach is limp. Stir in shrimp and distribute all ingredients evenly in pan. Beat eggs with water and pour over shrimp and spinach mixture. Do not stir, but cook over a low heat until set around the edges and on the bottom. Then place under a broiler for 2 to 3 minutes or until top is set and slightly browned. Cut into 4 wedges and serve with lime wedges and/or *Salsa Perejil* (page 31). Serves 4.

SALSA PEREJIL

(Parsley Sauce)

¼ cup olive oil	½ cup white wine vinegar
2 cups finely-chopped parsley	⅓ cup dry white wine
3 cloves garlic, mashed	¼ cup water or vegetable stock
1 tablespoon dried bread crumbs	1 teaspoon sugar
	½ teaspoon salt

Heat oil in small saucepan and sauté parsley and garlic until parsley is well softened. Stir in bread crumbs and cook 2 minutes. Add all other ingredients and simmer over a very low heat for 2 to 3 minutes. Remove from heat and cool. Serve at room temperature. Makes about 2 cups.

One dish from Tampico that has become famous throughout the republic is *Carne Asada a la Tampiqueña* (*Carne Asada* in the Tampico manner). This variation of the popular dish, *Carne Asada* (page 138) distinguishes itself when the grilled meat is served with *Enchiladas de Queso Blanco en Salsa Roja* (page 130), *Frijoles* (page 93), *Guacamole* (page 157), and sometimes, *rajas de chiles,* strips of *chile poblano* (see *chile poblano* preparation on page 33).

Tuxpan, about 100 miles south of Tampico, is another port city, although it is very low-keyed by comparison. It's a very pleasant-looking area with most of the city's activity located on the edge of the large Tuxpan river. It's also a sports fishing area, and I noticed a number of small commuter and pleasure boats crossing back and forth from the tree-lined banks.

Lunch there was relaxing. We ate at a small restaurant that had an enormous mango tree in the garden. It was the type that would have brought the Swiss Family Robinson to their knees. The sturdy branches were well-spaced and spread out in all directions. Mango trees are generally beautiful and often grow to be gigantic. Whenever I see one I am reminded of the time, some years ago, when I was visiting with some friends in the small patio of their house in Guanajuato. Suddenly, shattering the peace of the afternoon, there was a terrible clatter from a big mango tree several houses away. My hosts said, seriously, that there was a huge bird who lived in the tree and occasionally terrorized the children in the neighborhood. Here the real story ends, as I don't remember if I really saw that bird, or if the preposterousness of their description caused me to fantasize it. At any rate, I see it as a great yellow buzzard with long green headfeathers—a sort of poor man's *Quetzalcoatl*. As I write this I feel I really have gone beyond the facts, although I did hear it "chirp."

Back in the shade of the mango tree in Tuxpan we ate *Chiles Rellenos de Atún* (Tuna Stuffed Chiles). This was a new stuffing to me, with a touch of vinaigrette. I wanted to learn to make it and now after some experimentation I think my recipe tastes even better. It made a nice lunch that day with *Refritos* (Refried Beans, page 93), and warm, fresh corn *tortillas* (page 131).

CHILES RELLENOS DE ATÚN
(Tuna Stuffed Chiles)

8 large green chiles (not green peppers)—called *poblanos,* or use fresh California chiles or Anaheim chiles which are more common in the United States. Canned whole green chiles may be substituted and if used, disregard chile preparation instructions.

SAUCE:

4 teaspoons oil	2 tablespoons minced
½ small onion, minced	cilantro (optional)
2 cloves garlic, mashed	1 teaspoon lime juice
3 medium tomatoes, peeled, cored, and chopped	Salt

STUFFING:

⅓ cup minced onion	⅔ cup grated Monterey
1 tablespoon oil	Jack cheese
1 can (7-ounce) oil-packed tuna, well drained	¾ teaspoon oregano
	2 tablespoons lime juice
	Salt

BATTER

4 eggs, separated	¼ cup all-purpose flour
½ teaspoon salt	
¼ teaspoon baking powder	Oil for frying chiles

TO PREPARE CHILES: Put chiles on a baking pan 1 inch below broiler and blister them evenly, but do not let them get too limp. Put chiles in a plastic bag as they are ready and close the end of the bag so they can sweat. When they are cool enough to handle, carefully peel off thin outer skin with knife. Try not to tear them. (Do not remove stem end.) Cut a slit lengthwise in the chile stopping ¼ inch from either end and gently scoop out seeds. Rinse and dry well.

TO PREPARE SAUCE: Heat oil and sauté onions until limp. Add garlic, tomatoes, and cilantro, if desired, and simmer, covered, until sauce is well blended (about 15 minutes). Add lime juice and salt to taste.

TO MAKE STUFFING: Sauté onion in oil until limp and add tuna. Flake tuna and stir in cheese, oregano, and lime juice. Salt to taste.

TO MAKE BATTER: Beat whites of eggs with salt until they form soft, but definite peaks. Then beat yolks until they are thick and fold into whites. Mix baking powder and flour and carefully fold into eggs.

TO ASSEMBLE: Fill prepared chiles loosely with tuna stuffing. Secure split side with a toothpick. Heat about ¼ inch of oil in a frying pan. Dust each stuffed chile with a little flour, then coat chile very heavily with the batter. Fry in hot oil until lightly browned on each side. Set on paper towels to drain briefly. Serve chiles hot pouring hot tomato sauce over them just before serving. Serves 4.

Slightly over an hour south of Tuxpan is the town of Papantla, the vanilla center of Mexico and the home base of the colorful Totonac Indians. A tropical mountain valley hugs the town and the delicious aroma of vanilla pervades this area. The vanilla orchid was indigenous to this part of Mexico, and many years ago the Totonacs learned to cultivate it as a commercial crop. The early Spaniards first brought the vanilla pod to Europe and many a Spanish physician was convinced it was a healthful substance. In my opinion, vanilla is one of Mexico's finest gifts to cookery, and the town of Papantla smells so good that I wondered if the rainwater standing in the gutters was not from a great vanilla spill. Many little shops in town sell liquid vanilla, bean pods, vanilla liqueur, and little figures fashioned from the pods. But I didn't find the vanilla any cheaper there than elsewhere in Mexico, even though it all comes from Papantla.

The route south to the city of Veracruz is a beautiful drive, much like one would hope for in coastal Mexico—long, wide, sandy beaches, tall palm trees, soft breezes. Between the towns of Tecolutla and Nautla (the state of Veracruz is peppered with different Indian tribes and names of towns that make the tongue click) there are lovely beach homes, although most of them were closed up tight—perhaps from the recent storm. It's obvious that the climate is wild and unpredictable because most of the dwellings had storm shutters, and those close to the water were raised off the ground.

In 1839, the wife of the Spanish ambassador to New Spain, Frances Calderón de la Barca, wrote in *Life in Mexico* of her first impression of Veracruz.

"To me nothing can exceed the sadness of the aspect of this city and its environs—mountains of moving sand, formed by the violence of the north winds and which, by the reflection of the sun's rays, must greatly increase the suffocating heat of the atmosphere. The scene may resemble the ruins of Jerusalem, though without its sublimity."

Even though her first visit to Veracruz was in December, it is a city that is hot even in the so-called dead of winter. Still, I cannot believe that modern air conditioning alone could be responsible for my radically different first impression. I found Veracruz to be a beautiful city—all that I had expected and more. And what I saw in 1979 was the same city that Señora de la Barca had visited 140 years before, for the Spanish had built Veracruz as we see it today, although, of course, it is larger now.

What I did not expect was the strong Caribbean influence. Certainly the annual carnival costumes and music have strong Latin-Afro overtones, but the city itself is Caribbean in appearance. Tile roofs and ornate iron balconies and window guards add decorator touches to the building fronts. The main plaza is clean and well maintained, with shops and outdoor restaurants that serve all hours of the day and evening.

Here you can stop for a beer under the portals, have your shoes shined, and read the newspaper while listening to the marimba players or traveling street musicians. Veracruz is the home of the street harp, a small version of the classical harp. It can be carried while it is played and adds a special plaintive touch to the mariachi music played here.

Veracruz is well known for its aromatic coffee and fresh and varied seafood. Every restaurant has a multitude of fish choices only hours out of the Gulf, and the most famous regional dish is *Huachinango a la Veracruz* (Veracruz-style Red Snapper). It is an easy dish to duplicate, except for the extreme freshness of the fish and the large moist Mexican capers that are not available in the United States. When we were served this dish in Veracruz it was accompanied by a plate of *Arroz Blanco* (White Rice) and *Plátanos Fritos* (Fried Bananas).

Arroz Blanco is really not white but yellow rice that gets its color because the rice is sautéed in oil with onions until it turns yellow and then cooked in chicken broth which adds further to the color. The cooking bananas of Latin American and Caribbean cuisine are also known as plantains in English. They are larger than the bananas we know, and must be soft with black skins to be ripe for cooking. They are often available in Latin American markets, or a firm green banana can be substituted.

HUACHINANGO A LA VERACRUZ
(Veracruz-style Red Snapper)

1 4½ to 5 pound red snapper with head and tail	2 pounds tomatoes, peeled, cored and chopped
2 cloves garlic, mashed	1 bay leaf
2 tablespoons lime juice	½ teaspoon oregano
Salt	¼ teaspoon cinnamon
1 large onion, thinly sliced	½ teaspoon salt
4 tablespoons olive oil	2 tablespoons capers
2 cloves garlic, minced	Sliced lime
2 tablespoons minced parsley	⅓ cup pimiento-stuffed olives, sliced in halves

Have fish cleaned, wash well and dry. Rub inside with garlic and sprinkle with lime juice and salt. Set aside.

In a large frying pan, sauté onion in oil with garlic and parsley until softened. Add tomatoes, seasonings, and capers. Simmer for 15 minutes or until well blended. Place fish in a large casserole or baking dish and pour sauce over it. Bake in slow (300° oven) for about 50 minutes or until fish is no longer transparent and flakes easily with a fork. Turn once during the baking. Transfer whole fish to a platter, pour hot sauce over it, then garnish with lime slices and olives. Serve with *Arroz a la Mexicana* (page 22) and warm corn *tortillas* (page 131). Serves 4 to 5.

ARROZ BLANCO
(White Rice)

2 cups long-grain white
rice
Hot water
½ cup oil
½ large onion, finely
chopped

2 cloves garlic, mashed
4 cups well-salted
chicken broth

Pour rice in a bowl, cover with hot water and let sit for 15 minutes. Drain and rinse with cold water until water is clear of starch. In a heavy-bottomed pot heat oil and well-drained rice. Stir and coat rice with hot oil. Fry rice over a high heat, stirring frequently until rice begins to turn yellow. Add onion and garlic and continue to stir and fry until rice is golden yellow. Reduce heat to simmer, and pour chicken broth over rice and stir once to settle. Steam for about 20 minutes or until all liquid is absorbed and rice is tender. Serves 5 to 6.

PLÁTANOS FRITOS
(Fried Bananas)

3 large, soft, black-
skinned plantains (firm
green bananas can be
substituted)

Flour
Oil or chicken fat

Peel plantains and slice in ½-inch lengths. Roll in flour and fry in hot oil or chicken fat until golden brown. Serve with *Arroz Blanco*. Serves 6.

Veracruz is the oldest city in Mexico and the major maritime link with Europe. It is where Cortés first landed, and where he burned his ships so his men would have to push on inland instead of returning to Spain. Its history is fraught with invasions from foreign powers and more than once the city has sustained major damage. It is remarkable that it still welcomes the traveler.

One of the historical curiosities in Veracruz is the Fortress of San Juan de Ulua. Located on an island in the harbor, this moated and medieval structure was built in the early sixteenth century to defend the port of Veracruz, but was later used as a prison. It was most crowded during the Inquisition which prevailed in New Spain (Mexico) as well as Isabella's Spain. And it is rather worth the horrible and fascinating tour.

There is some confusion about the origin of the name *Ulua*. Some say it is a corruption of the Indian God's name, *Alcohua*, but I prefer our guide's explanation. When the Spaniard, Juan de Grijalva, arrived on the little island a year before Cortés, the Indians paddled out to meet him, calling *"kalua, kalua"* which meant "welcome." Grijalva's sea ears understood the greeting as *"ulua!"*

We had a guide who insisted on speaking English. He had a prepared speech and I think he liked the way it sounded. When we would interrupt him with a question, he would answer in Spanish or English, backtracking a couple of paragraphs so we would not lose the chronology. Like many contemporary Mexican men, he wore dark glasses, even in the darkest of dungeons. He must have had the layout memorized, and was determined to lead us into every corner. I could't see a thing much of the time and was very skittish about going into those terrible little cells that still smelled of despair, especially when the limestone floors were slimy with condensation. "Just a little bit further," and he would pull me by the hand when I hung back. He was very anti-Spanish and anti-Spanish clergy, although he was very obviously *meztizo* (Spanish and Indian).

Back into the airy beauty of the city, the long *malecón* (beach sidewalk) is well worth a stroll or drive. The street is wide and clean and the water blue-green and serene. There are quite a number of new homes along this road as well as many old and new hotels with good dining rooms. We stopped to have lunch in a spacious and gracious hotel restaurant, and filled up on a magnificent *Sopa de Marisco,* (Seafood Soup) that was served with slices of lime and minced fresh, green chiles. Mexicans use limes on practically everything and fish is always accompanied with it. You will even see children in the streets squeezing lime on hot, plain corn *tortillas*. Lemons are not common in Mexico, but limes are grown in all warm areas. They are cut lengthwise for better juicing, and the sturdy metal, hand lime squeezer is one of my favorite gifts to bring back to the States.

SOPA DE MARISCOS
(Seafood Soup)

4 tablespoons olive oil
1 large onion, thinly
  sliced
3 cloves garlic, minced
1 quart rich fish broth or
  bottled clam juice
3 cups water
2 tablespoons red wine
  vinegar
2 pounds tomatoes,
  peeled, cored, and
  puréed in blender
2 bay leaves
2 sprigs of fresh thyme or
  1 teaspoon dried

1 teaspoon oregano
Salt and pepper
2 pounds fresh sea bass,
  trimmed and cut into 2-
  inch pieces
1 dozen fresh large
  prawns
1 dozen fresh oysters with
  liquid
1 dozen clams, well
  scrubbed
Lime wedges
Fresh *chile jalapeño*,
  chopped

Heat oil in large, heavy-bottomed soup pot and sauté onions until limp. Add garlic to pot as onions are softening. Add fish or clam broth, water, vinegar, puréed tomatoes, bay leaves, thyme, and oregano. Cover and simmer for ½ hour and then salt and pepper to taste. Add bass, prawns, and oysters. Simmer, uncovered, until bass flakes with fork and prawns turn pink. Meanwhile, in a separate pot steam clams in small amount of water. Put 2 clams in each soup bowl and ladle in hot soup and fish. Serve with lime wedges, chopped fresh *chile jalapeño* and warm *bolillos* (page 18). Serves 6.

CHAPTER THREE

The Yucatán Peninsula

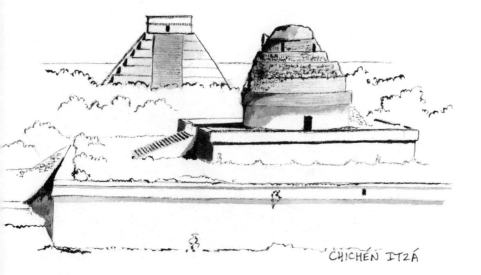

CHICHÉN ITZÁ

VILLAHERMOSA means "beautiful town." As the capital of the state of Tabasco it's a rather nice short stop, although it's certainly every bit as hot as the sauce during most of the year. The city is located on the banks of the huge Grijalva River, and has been greatly modernized in the last few years— at least compared with Graham Greene's response when he visited Villahermosa in 1938.

Nothing to do but drink gassy fruit drinks (no miracle in this Godless state will turn this aerated water into wine) and watch the horrifying abundance of just life. You can't open a book without a tiny scrap of life scuttling across the page; the stalls are laden with great pulpy tasteless fruits, and when the light comes out, so do the beetles; the pavement by the sour green riverside is black with them. You kill them on your bedroom floor, and by morning as I have said, they have been drained away by more life—hordes of ants that come up between the tiles at the scent of death or sweetness.

With this description in mind, I looked over the city rather carefully on my first trip through. What the traveler sees now are streets that are wide and well maintained, and, for the most part, they are clean. A pretty riverside boulevard invites strolling and sitting, especially under the lamplight on balmy evenings. The city is the hub of the oil industry which accounts for the new growth and apparent prosperity.

Culturally, Villahermosa has two strong attractions, La Venta Museum and the Tabasco Museum of Archaeology. The first is an outdoor archaeological exhibition of giant Olmec carvings found in the nearby oil digs. The Olmecs are thought to predate all Mexican Indians and seemed to have a fancy for large head sculptures. The Archaeology Museum is considered to be one of the finest in all of Mexico and has a sizable collection of artifacts from the Mayas as well as the Olmec and Toltec civilizations.

True, the heat can still be blinding, the mosquitos are no less active than they were in 1938, and the edges of the town have that grime that is so common to oil centers, but Villahermosa is probably not a place where a tourist would want to spend much time anyway. For most of the passers-through, it is the crossroad to the Yucatán. Either one turns northeast to the Island of Carmen and the Bay of Campeche, or east to the state of Quintana Roo and the Caribbean. It is also the principal transportation terminal to the Mayan ruins of Palenque.

Palenque is a bit out of the way for the auto traveler. The road into the ruins is also the only route back to the highway, although it is straight and easy. Once, however, it was only accessible by muleback, a long and arduous trip through difficult weather and thick jungle. The nonarchaeological distinction between these Palenque ruins and the Mayan sites in the Yucatán is the density of the jungle and the dampness. Palenque is said to be the rainiest spot in Mexico, and truly there is a constant moisture that clings to your clothes and bed sheets. The ground around the ruins sinks under your feet and the sky always looks as if it it's going to rain or it just quit. One of the great mysteries of the Mayas is why did they so frequently and abruptly abandon their developing cities and strike out for a new location. Some scholars muse that it was because there are no rivers or lakes in the Yucatán and the rainfall is so unpredictable. Surely this would have been the reverse at Palenque—they were probably sick of the wet and tired of hacking back the creeping jungle. It is more than likely that the Mayas were constantly seeking new cornfields since the cultivation of maize or corn was a major agricultural responsibility for all Central American Indians. It was a staple food, yet one of the most abusive crops known to soil.

At any rate, no one answers the doors of Palenque now and the abandoned city is very overgrown. It is a wonderful view, though, and the Great Palace, the most prominent structure, is a child's delight of endless corridors, precarious walkways, and dead-end rooms. Next to it is the Temple of Inscriptions, a perfectly constructed pyramid topped with a temple that is etched with yet-to-be-understood hieroglyphics. About thirty years ago, researchers were led to believe there was more underneath, and diggings and movings uncovered a sizable tomb with skeletons of a noble and his guard servants, along with many treasures. The most prized was a jade mask that is now in the Museum of Anthropology in Mexico City.

Back on the highway, toward the eastern side of the Yucatán Peninsula and the long state of Quintana Roo, the traveler begins to get a feel of the terrain. The area is remote as it is a true peninsula, waterlocked by the Gulf of Mexico and Caribbean Sea. And landward, for a long time, it was separated from the rest of Mexico by dense jungle and a choking climate. The early Yucatán settlers had much more in common with Europe and Cuba than with Mexico. This and the strong influence of the Mayas is what accounts for the unique cuisine of the area.

Yucatán cooking is distinguished by the use of a number of ingredients that are not common to most of Mexico, although in southern Mexico there are some similarities. As mentioned in the Introduction, regional cooking is less of an issue now because of the advances in communication and transportation. Still there are some foods that are specific to certain sections of the country. The Yucatán is probably the most independent.

Anchiote, the pungent seed of the tropical annatto tree, is used both as a flavoring and coloring in Yucatán dishes. These seeds are very hard and must be soaked and softened to be used. Generally, they are made into a paste, and in many markets in the region, this paste can be purchased already prepared.

Banana leaves are used for wrapping tamales, meats, and fowl while steaming and baking, and also while grilling as open-fire cooking is common to the Yucatán. Epazote, a leafy herb, is another favorite ingredient, although it is also used in other areas of the country. It certainly adds the right touch to black beans. The delicious black bean, the *frijol negro,* is eaten throughout the Caribbean islands and in southern Mexico, especially around Oaxaca. This delectable rich bean, undoubtedly my favorite and widely used throughout the Yucatán.

The bitter Seville orange is peculiar to the peninsula. It is the variety we know as the marmalade orange, but in the Yucatán it adds just the right touch to sauced dishes. The Seville is not a juice orange, and I have heard that some groups of Mayas will not use it at all, fearing it will cause sterility in women. Also, there is a sour lime grown in the Yucatán and used in special dishes, most commonly *Sopa de Lima,* a chicken-based soup with lime.

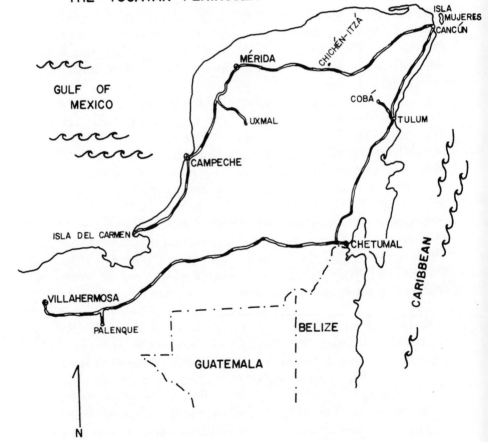

THE YUCATÁN PENINSULA

Fish, of course, is popular on the edges of the peninsula. Pork is used as it is in other areas of Mexico. There are many Yucatán recipes using *venado* (venison)—probably originating with the small red deer that is part of the fauna of the area. Chicken and turkey dishes are popular, although wild turkey, the original ingredient, is not the common source anymore.

At the southeastern corner of the peninsula is Chetumal, the capital city of Quintana Roo and the last Mexican stop before the intrepid traveler enters Belize. Until very recently Chetumal was isolated by not having good roads, trains or air travel into the city, with a rugged coastline on the Caribbean side. Once it was reported to be only a stop for smugglers and *chicleros,* the rugged, lawless workers who gathered the sap of the Yucatán's abundant chicle trees. Chicle is the chewy base for gum which explains why gum is called *chicle* in Mexico, and is obviously the origin of the name of our Chicklet gum.

I liked Chetumal, although is seemed like two cities. The interior is a bustling center for commerce because Quintana Roo is a free port state. Block after block of the downtown is filled with shops with the most eclectic stock—Japanese cameras, Belgian lace, French perfumes, German machinery, and Italian gowns. Since the rest of Mexico is forced to pay outrageous duty in imports this city is continually packed with buyers from all over the republic. Cancún, the new slick resort town 230 miles north, also has a number of duty-free shops, but the emphasis there is on French and Italian fashion. Chetumal is more fun because the goods are so varied. It is also a popular vacation town for Mexicans which means it is crowded and lively at night.

The older section by the water presents the other side of Chetumal. There the look is Caribbean with well-kept white wooden buildings and well-tended lawns. The waterfront has a nice promenade and most of the good fish restaurants are in this area. Here we sampled *Pámpano a la Yucateca* (Yucatán-style Pámpano), tender fish fillets prepared in an anchiote marinade. Pámpano is not readily available in the rest of North America, but flounder works very well in this recipe.

PÁMPANO A LA YUCATECA

(Yucatán-Style Pámpano)

1½ teaspoons anchiote
   (annatto tree seeds)
1 teaspoon oregano
3 large cloves garlic
2 tablespoons olive oil
Juice of 1 large lime
12 whole cumin seeds
⅓ teaspoon salt

Dash of cayenne pepper
1½ pounds pámpano or
   flounder fillets
1 large onion, chopped
2 tablespoons oil
1 cup thinly-sliced
   zucchini
Lime wedges

Cover anchiote with water and simmer for 5 minutes. Leave to soak for at least 8 hours. Drain and smash seeds a little with spoon or pestle and put in the blender with oregano, garlic, oil, lime juice, cumin, and salt. Blend as smooth as possible. Add a little cayenne to taste. Spread fish in a baking dish and brush anchiote mixture on both sides. Marinate for 2 hours.

Just before broiling fish, sauté onion in oil until softened and slightly golden. When onions are almost sautéed, add zucchini to pan, and place fish dish under the broiler (about 3 inches from flame) until fish flakes easily. It is not necessary to turn fish but do not overcook. (If the fish exudes a lot of juice during the broiling, spoon it off as it should not stew, but should not be dry either.) Remove from broiler, top with sautéed onions and zucchini and serve with several lime wedges. This is good with *Arroz Blanco* (page 37). Serves 4.

Traveling north on the reasonably new and decent road along the Quintana Roo coast, I was slightly disappointed at not being able to see the water. Unfortunately, the eastern coastline of the Yucatán is jagged and subject to tidal changes, storms, and hurricanes. I had expected the entire peninsula to be more like the South Pacific islands with lush tropical valleys, but it is flat as a pancake and the foliage along the side of the road was mostly scrubby and dusty. (However, I didn't mind that too much as I have an unexplained fondness for Mexican dust.)

In reality, this strand between the road and the Caribbean is a dense jungle, thick with mosquitos, ticks, poisonous snakes, exotic birds, and sloshed with marshes. The Mayas had to be a plucky lot to survive those conditions, and apparently they did. Many ruins along the coast were sighted by early ships on the Carribbean. Other sites have been discovered and mapped only in the last twenty years.

Geologically, the Yucatán peninsula is a thin layer of soil over a limestone bed that has many underground rivers and wells. Some of these pools break through the hard crust, and are referred to as *cenotes* by the Mayas. They were considered sacred and the big, limestone-ringed *cenote* at the famous Mayan city of Chichén-Itzá was where many beautiful maidens were thrown to their death as sacrifices to the rain God, *Chac.*

Tulum is the one Mayan ruin on the coast that is accessible to tourists. This was the city Juan Grijalva, the pre-Cortés explorer, saw from his ship and likened to Seville in Spain. But its grandeur frightened him, and both he and Cortés deliberately sailed around the peninsula for Veracruz after they saw Tulum.

Certainly it must have been startling for the early Spanish explorers to come upon structures such as the Mayas built. Walking around Tulum one cannot help but marvel at the sense of magnificence in all of their architecture. What especially impressed me was the height of their walls and buildings, and the distance between steps favored by a race so small in stature. Even the Mayas of today are smaller than most Central American Indians.

Inland from Tulum are the ruins of Cobá, still very much unearthed. This may turn out to be the grandest of all Mayan archaeological sites having, among other features, six full pyramids, although most of them have not been excavated. It gave me a strange feeling to think that there could be buildings and artifacts still undiscovered under my feet.

The ancient Mayan Yucatán was a city state. Unlike the American Indian whose instinct was to live and move with the rhythm of nature, the Indians of Central America were concerned with building stationary empires and in conquering nature. The Mayas may have linked all their cities with roads;

it is thought that the great arch at Kabah was the entrance to a ceremonial road that led to Cobá, sixty miles east. This arch, incidentally, was engineered in the Mayan fashion of placing layers of overlapping stones closer together as they neared the desired peak. They had no knowledge of the classic keystone arch. Nor did the Mayas appear to have any notion of the wheel, and they did not use any metal. (Their cutting tools were made of obsidian.) Yet they evolved a complex and accurate calendar. Their astronomers were so efficient that they not only recorded movements and positions of the planets, but also the eclipses of the sun and phases of the moon, and they could predict future ones. Moreover, their system of mathematics included a zero for making calculations. They were, perhaps, hundreds of years before Europe in this concept.

In addition, the Mayas believed in baptism, penance, the Eucharist (they baked a doll of flour and distributed it), circumcision, and places of eternal punishment or reward. The latter was related to comfort and desirable climatic conditions. Obviously, the opposite was full of hurricanes and mosquitoes as big as bullets.

My mind was constantly on the Mayas while we were in the Yucatán, but driving away from the silent, yet uncovered Cobá and the heavy heat of the interior, Cancún seemed like it would be a welcome reprieve. Certainly this is the most nonhistorical, noncultural spot in the area.

Cancún cannot really be considered Mexican. It is a lovely resort, but it is so glossy and modern that the traveler is startled to hear Spanish spoken. The islands of Cozumel, south of Cancún, and Isla Mujeres, slightly north, are also resorts, although they do claim some ruins. (Isla Mujeres, the Island of Women, is so named because of the Mayan female statues that were found in the temple there.)

Cancún is mostly a long strand of sand covered with high-rise hotels, white beaches, and spare, but stately palm trees. The weather is wonderful and the feeling is all luxury. Caribbean water is beautiful—warm and stunningly green and clear. In fact, the waters around Cozumel are supposed to be about the clearest in the world due to the strong currents that brush along that coastline.

Cancún has become one of the great watering holes of the country. All along the coastline of Mexico, fancy and exotic drinks are available—specialties of the particular areas. Since Cuba is only a whistle away from Cancún, some of the rum drinks have drifted across the waters. White rum and dry vermouth is the popular Latin version of a not-so-dry martini, sometimes called *Cóctel Presidente* (President's Cocktail). It's a nice slow drink served with a bowl of *cacahuates con limón,* which is nothing more than shelled peanuts with lime juice squeezed over them.

CÓCTEL PRESIDENTE
(President's Cocktail)

1½ ounces of white rum
¼ ounce dry vermouth

Mix rum and vermouth together in a 6 ounce tumbler filled with ice. Serve with a twist of lime. Makes 1 drink.

Traveling west from Cancún to Mérida we stopped first at Chichén-Itzá, an archaeological study that clearly represents the new and old Mayan empires. The older section is south of the road, and the "New Chichén" is to the north, although both parts contain structures of both eras. It is interesting how this city looms up, so out of place, on either side of a modern highway. The simple Mayan homes of today are oval shaped with thatched roofs and are found all over the Yucatán. The contrast between these primitive but modern dwellings and the ancient but glorious buildings of the past make Chichén-Itzá one of the most interesting anachronisms of Mexico.

Walking just a few steps off the highway we came face to face with *El Castillo* (The Castle), a pyramid with ninety-one steps.

After another little jaunt we were in the great ball court. It is said that the Toltecs introduced this sport and that it had religious significance. The court is 272 feet long and 100 feet wide, and there is a circular stone with a hole in it, twenty-seven feet up on each side. The players, using every part of their body except their hands, were to get a small, hard ball through that hole. The winners received lavish gifts while the losers became sacrificial victims almost immediately. It was, what one would call, "a serious game."

It's a never-ending curiosity to me why Mexican archaeological sites are so haphazardly maintained. It can be explained in part because Mexicans are the chief "litter bugs" of the continent, and the advent of plastic containers and bags has done a great disservice to the appearance of the countryside. As yet, Mexico hasn't launched a clean-up campaign—at least one that amounts to anything. (It must be a touch of truth as well as whimsy that inspired the name "City Dump" for one of Puerto Vallarta's popular discos.)

It is not uncommon to slip on fruit peels or candy wrappers or stumble over a beer can at the foot of one of Mexico's most impressive pyramids. On the other hand, almost nothing is "off limits." If you want to rest, you can sit down on the belly of one of the numerous *chacmool* figures that lie around the sites (probably where lay the heads of sacrificial victims). In fact, the only restricted areas seem to be those where officials are afraid you may not be able to find your way out or back.

Chichén-Itzá has its share of good hotels and restaurants and it was here that we tasted the famous Yucatán *Sopa de Lima* (Lime Soup), a tangy bowl of chicken, giblets, and vegetables, flavored with the sour lime of the area. It can also be made with sweet lime and some lemon or grapefruit peel. After all, your guests won't know the difference if they haven't had the real McCarlos.

SOPA DE LIMA

(Lime Soup)

2½ to 3 pound whole
    chicken with giblets
2½ quarts water
1½ teaspoons salt
  4 chicken livers
  4 chicken gizzards
  2 cups water
1½ tablespoons chicken
    fat or lard
  1 small onion, halved
    and thinly sliced
  1 small, green pepper,
    thinly sliced
  3 large cloves garlic,
    minced

¼ teaspoon oregano
  2 medium tomatoes,
    peeled and chopped
Juice of 2 sweet limes
  2 pieces of grapefruit
    peel—2 inches long
    and 1 inch wide
Salt and pepper
  8 stale tortillas, thinly
    sliced
Chicken fat or lard
Chopped *chiles serranos*
Lime wedges

Remove giblets from chicken and retain liver and gizzard for later. Cut chicken in half and put in a soup pot with water. Bring to a boil, add salt and reduce heat to simmer. Cover and simmer until meat is tender and falls from the bone (about 2½ hours). Strain off broth and chill. Remove meat from bones and skin.

When fat has set on top of chilled broth, remove and save for sautéeing.

Put all chicken livers and giblets in broth and bring to a boil. Simmer for 15 minutes and remove with a slotted spoon. Trim gristle from gizzards, chop with livers into small pieces and return along with chicken to soup pot. Add 2 cups of water.

In hot fat or lard, sauté onions with green pepper, garlic, and oregano until onions are limp. Add to soup pot along with tomatoes, lime juice, and grapefruit peel. Simmer, covered, for an hour and salt and pepper to taste. Just before serving, fry tortilla strips in hot fat or lard until crisp. Divide strips among 4 to 6 soup bowls and cover with hot soup. Serve with small bowls of chopped chiles and lime wedges. Serves 4 to 6.

Mérida is a large city, clean and airy with lots of magnolia and laurel trees. (Laurel leaves are used to flavor Yucatán cooking.) The streets are long and narrow and the houses have nice iron grillwork in the Caribbean style. The city has abundant parks and plazas, the most famous being the *Plaza de la Independencia,* a central location from which the traveler can walk to the big market and to most of Mérida's historical buildings.

This is a city influenced by Europeans and the distinctions still prevail—a complementary contrast between the small, tidy, round-headed Mayas and the slender, olive-skinned Spanish descendents. The very common Mayan dress, a loose shift with embroidery around the neck, is called the *huipal* and is very popular with hotel and restaurant employees who wear them like uniforms. These are the dresses that tourists like to bring home.

And in Mérida, because it is so hot, businessmen are most comfortable in *guayabera* shirts which are tailored, but tucked and embroidered, too. Worn outside of trousers, the look is definitely associated with the tropics. Méridanos on their way to work in the morning, wearing dark glasses and *guayabera* shirts, swinging their briefcases, are the most comfortable-looking businessmen in the world.

I had heard that Mérida was not known for particularly good restaurants, but that was not what we discovered. There are many small, inexpensive places that serve traditional Maya-Spanish dishes that are wonderful treats for the tourist.

I loved the *Huevos Motuleños* (eggs Motul-style), a popular breakfast dish of the area. The recipe originated in the nearby town of Motul, not far from Mérida, and is a wonderful introduction to the *frijol negro*. In Motul, the good cooks had the notion to fry cooked beans into a paste to be spread on corn tortillas and topped with chopped ham, fried eggs, and a fresh tomato sauce. Delicious!

One very interesting dish, peculiar to the Yucatán, is the *Queso Relleno* (Stuffed Cheese). Because Quintana Roo is a free port state, Dutch cheeses can be purchased rather reasonably—certainly more cheaply than in the United States. Therefore, you may find this rather costly for a first course or appetizer (as it is usually served). I'm still curious to know how this recipe evolved, aside from the fact that stuffed foods are popular in Mexican cuisine. Maybe the size of a big cheese was just too overwhelming or uninteresting alone. Anyway, it is a very delicious dish, not difficult to prepare, but a bit time-consuming.

QUESO RELLENO
(Stuffed Cheese)

1 4-pound Edam cheese, round or loaf	1 tablespoon each capers and raisins
1½ pounds lean pork (after trimming)	1 fresh *chile jalapeño,* cored and minced
3 cups water	1 tablespoon red wine vinegar
3 cloves garlic, mashed	10 whole peppercorns
1 teaspoon oregano	2 whole cloves
½ teaspoon salt	Salt to taste
4 eggs, hardboiled	Oil
2 tablespoons oil	Cheesecloth
1 small onion, minced	1 large tomato, peeled and puréed in a blender
½ small, green pepper, minced	Pinch saffron
1 large tomato, peeled and puréed in a blender	2 tablespoons flour
1 dozen green olives, pitted and chopped	16 to 20 corn tortillas

Peel the wax off the cheese and cut a ½-inch slice off the top to serve as a lid, so the cheese can be hollowed out. With a knife and spoon remove the insides of the cheese leaving a ½-inch shell all around and on the bottom. (Save the cheese that is removed for other uses.) Set cheese shell aside.

Cut meat into ½-inch cubes and put into a pot with water, garlic, oregano and salt. Simmer covered for ½ hour or until tender. Meanwhile, peel eggs. Keep yolks whole and set aside. Chop whites and set aside.

When meat is almost tender, heat oil in a frying pan and sauté onions and pepper until softened. Add tomato purée, olives, capers, raisins, chopped chile, chopped egg white, and vinegar. Grind peppercorns and cloves in spice grinder or mortar and add to mixture in frying pan. Simmer mixture for 3 to 4 minutes. Remove cooked meat from broth and retain broth. Chop meat finely and add to frying pan. Heat all ingredients through and salt to taste. Spoon some of this mixture into the hollowed cheese and then set in whole egg yolks. Fill with remaining mixture and set the cheese lid on top. Oil the outside of the cheese well, wrap in a large piece of cheesecloth and tie securely. Place in a steamer above water and steam over a medium heat for about 15 minutes, or until cheese softens and begins to spread. Meanwhile, reheat broth with puréed tomato and add a pinch of saffron. Remove ½ cup of broth mixture, mix in blender with flour and return to pot. Stir until gravy thickens slightly. Remove stuffed cheese from cloth and transfer to a serving platter. Pour gravy over cheese and serve with spoons—scooping cheese and filling into warmed corn tortillas. Serves 8 to 10.

HUEVOS MOTULEÑOS

(Eggs Motul-style)

1½ medium onion finely chopped
1 3-inch green chile
2 tablespoons oil
3 large tomatoes, peeled and chopped
Salt
Bacon fat or lard
8 corn tortillas

2 cups fried black beans (page 93)
1 cup diced cooked ham
4 large eggs, fried
4 tablespoons grated Parmesan cheese

Make *salsa* by sautéing onions and chile in oil until well softened. Add tomatoes and cook over a low heat until well blended. Set aside.

In bacon fat or lard fry tortillas until crisp. Spread 4 tortillas with hot fried beans and sprinkle with diced ham.* Top each mixture with a fried egg (or 2 if the appetite demands). Then cover each egg with remaining tortillas. Heat *salsa* until very hot, spoon over each portion and top with grated cheese. Serves 4.

* Sometimes cooked peas are sprinkled on the beans with the ham.

Like many areas of Mexico, the Yucatán has its special chicken dish—*Pollo Píbil* (Chicken in a Banana Leaf). Chicken pieces are marinated in a paste of anchiote, cumin and Seville orange juice, then baked or grilled wrapped in pieces of banana leaf. The banana leaf does add to the special flavor of this dish, but I have used large chard leaves also. While it is not the same, it is very good, necessity being the mother of chard in this instance. The directions here are for both leaves as you may be able to get banana leaves at a Latin-American grocery store or, possibly, from a nearby banana tree.

POLLO PÍBIL
(Chicken in a Banana Leaf)

2 teaspoons anchiote seed
¼ teaspoon whole cumin seed
¼ teaspoon dried oregano
1 teaspoon salt
4 large cloves garlic
6 peppercorns

4 tablespoons Seville orange juice or 2 tablespoons each lemon and orange juice
Dash hot pepper sauce
2½ to 3 pound chicken, quartered
⅓ cup oil

1 large onion, thinly sliced	or about 6 large Swiss chard leaves and 4
2 large tomatoes, sliced	bay leaves
4 pieces of banana leaf for wrapping chicken	Salt to taste

Cover anchiote seeds with water and simmer for 5 minutes, then soak for at least 8 hours. Mash seed slightly with a spoon and put into the blender with cumin, oregano, salt, garlic, peppercorns, juice, and hot pepper sauce. Blend into as smooth a paste as possible. Dry chicken parts well and spread all but 2 teaspoons anchiote mixture on all sides of chicken. Cover and marinate for 8 hours in the refrigerator.

Heat oil in frying pan and sauté onions with remaining anchiote mixture until onions are limp and yellow. Remove from pan and sauté tomato slices briefly. If you are using banana leaves, sear them first over a flame so they soften to bend and place 1 piece of chicken on 1 piece of leaf, meaty side down. Distribute onions and tomato slices over chicken and wrap securely with the leaves. Place chicken in a covered casserole and bake at 325° for 30 minutes, then unwrap and turn pieces up. Spoon drippings over vegetables and continue to bake, unwrapped and uncovered, until done (about 30 or more minutes).

If you are using Swiss chard leaves, cover bottom of a 9 x 13-inch baking dish with 3 chard leaves and place chicken pieces meaty side down. Spread onions, tomato slices, and bay leaves over chicken, then cover with the remaining chard. Salt lightly and cover tightly with lid or foil. Place in 325° oven for 30 minutes, then push chard leaves aside and turn chicken meaty side up. Spoon vegetables and drippings over chicken and bake, uncovered, until done (about 30 more minutes).

Serve with *Arroz Blanco* (*page 37*). Serves 4.

Another popular dish from the Yucatán that is served in Mérida is *panuchos,* tortillas that are allowed to puff up while they are cooking so they can be stuffed. The common stuffing is a paste of fried black beans and hard-boiled eggs. After they are stuffed, they are lightly fried and garnished with a mixture of shredded pork, chicken or turkey, and pickled onion rings. They are very substantial appetizers or they can be served as a first course. Make them early in the day and then fry them when your guests arrive. And if you have not made tortillas often, do not be surprised if your first attempt looks as amateurish as mine did. They'll taste good anyway!

PANUCHOS CON PAVO
(Stuffed Tortillas with Turkey)

GARNISH:

2 cups shredded turkey meat
2 medium onions, thinly sliced
1 cup white wine vinegar

¼ cup water
1½ teaspoons salt
6 cumin seeds
¼ teaspoon oregano
2 bay leaves
Dash cayenne pepper

FILLING:

2 cups beans (*Frijoles,* page 93)

2 hard-boiled eggs, crumbled

Tortilla recipe (page 131)
⅔ cup lard, shortening or oil for frying

Prepare the garnish the day before. Shred the turkey and slice the onions. Mix together vinegar, water, salt, and seasonings and mix with onions. Cover and refrigerate. (The turkey can also be mixed in the pickling onions or stored separately.)

Put beans through a meat grinder, food mill, or in a blender. Grind to a smooth paste and put in a small frying pan to be heated before stuffing.

Make tortilla dough according to recipe. This should make about 20 balls, 1 inch in diameter. (This gives you some extra dough to fail with—try to get 14 successful stuffers.) A frying pan or griddle should be lightly greased and heated over a high-medium flame or coil. Press tortilla balls into circles about 4 inches in diameter. (See instructions for pressing and cooking on page 132.) When tortilla nears its cooked stage it usually puffs up, but you can help by pressing slightly on the tortilla. Remove from heat and cool for a few seconds and then make an incision in the puffed skin ¼ of an inch in from the edge and about ⅓ around the tortilla. (Be careful not to puncture the underside of the tortilla.) Put 3 to 4 teaspoons of the heated beans in the pocket and a little of the crumbled eggs. Flatten the top to seal and keep stuffed *panuchos* covered with a slightly damp cloth. Repeat process until you have 14 stuffed tortillas.

Heat 3 tablespoons lard, shortening or oil at a time in heavy-bottomed skillet and fry 3 to 4 *panuchos* at a time until they are just a little crisp around the edges. Repeat until all are fried, then serve garnished with shredded turkey and pickled onions. Makes 14 *panuchos.*

From Mérida it is less than two hours to Uxmal, a Mayan archaeological site that ranks with Chichén-Itzá in importance, although it is different even to the untrained eye. While Chichén-Itzá was built by Toltec-Mayan cultures, Uxmal is pure Maya with a long historical heyday (600 to 1000 A.D.). The structures have a geometric beauty, and it is said that the precise elegance of the Palace of the Governors was the architectural inspiration for the National Museum of Anthropology in Mexico City.

The highway through Campeche on the western side passes through a number of *henequén* fields. *Henequén* or sisal is an agave plant (tequilla comes from the same plant family) that grows without irrigation and whose thick leaves yield a fiber for making rope and woven goods. The sisal industry was once the major source of wealth in the Yucatán, but this has changed because of the competition from other growing areas and the development of plastics. Still, there are numerous small roadside stands selling locally produced *henequén* products—a cottage industry of place mats, baskets, hats, etc. (We heard the production of indoor/outdoor carpet is utilizing *henequén,* but it is unlikely that the synthetic world of the future will allow for a new summit in sisal.)

The city of Campeche is the seafood center of the Yucatán peninsula, and it is a bright and shining, white capital. Once the city was completely walled to protect the residents from pirates but still the scoundrels managed to carry off many beautiful maidens. Those walls are down now, although there is a small sea wall. South of the main part of the city, the *marineros* (sailors) sit, mend their nets, and putter around their small fishing boats.

Campeche restaurants specialize in fish of the area—black snapper, shark, crab, shrimp, and oysters. A splendid lunch break is a *Cóctel Campechana Marinera* (Shrimp and Oyster Cocktail), a chilled, spicy combination of both Gulf favorites.

CÓCTEL CAMPECHANA MARINERA
(Campeche Shrimp and Oyster Cocktail)

All ingredients should be chilled before mixing.

16 shrimp cooked and shelled
16 small oysters, raw (or 8 large and cut in half)
2 cups tomato juice
¼ cup dry vermouth
2 tablespoons lime juice
1 teaspoon Worcestershire Sauce
2 tablespoons grated onion
Salt and hot pepper sauce to taste
Lime wedges, fresh ground pepper

Divide shrimp and oysters among 4 appetizer cocktail glasses. Mix together tomato juice, vermouth, lime juice, Worcestershire Sauce and grated onion. Add salt and hot pepper sauce to taste and pour mixture over seafood. Serve with lime wedges and fresh ground pepper. Serves 4.

Less that 150 miles south of Campeche lies Isla del Carmen (Island of Carmen), only accessible to the mainland by ferry lines at either end of the island. My brother and I had heard the most sublime description of this slender piece of earth bordered by sandy beaches and lapping surf, and heavily dotted with coconut palms, so we looked forward to our visit. And indeed the drive along the Campeche coast to the ferry stop at Isla Aguada was serene and tropical.

Not much has changed in Carmen since that description was registered. It's still a sleepy island town with very little new construction and only two hotels. And it still has good seafood and unpretentious restaurants on the water. But the ferry traffic has multiplied mightily since the oil boom. Some of the richest fields are in the water off Carmen, and there is no question that in time this relaxed little island will feel the effects of the petroleum industry.

Meanwhile, the shrimp fried in *masa* batter was delicious, and the activity in the town easy and lighthearted. We spent a lovely long evening with some engineers (oil again) from the city of Campeche, eating oysters and shrimp, and listening to them sing and play on their guitars some of the most beautiful *corridas* (folk songs) of Mexico. I was reminded of Frances Calderón de la Barca who said of Mexico, "Fine voices are said to be extremely common, as is natural in a country peopled from Spain . . ." Certainly the evening in Carmen served as a warm and memorable good-bye to the Yucatán.

CAMARONES FRITOS DE CARMEN

(Fried Shrimp of Carmen)

20 large shrimp	¼ teaspoon baking
3 eggs, separated	powder
½ cup milk	½ cup *masa harina**
¼ teaspoon salt	Oil or lard
⅛ teaspoon cayenne	
pepper	

*corn flour

Shell and devein shrimp, but do not remove tail. Beat egg yolks with milk. Combine seasonings, baking powder and *masa* and stir into milk and egg mixture. Beat whites stiff and fold into *masa* mixture to make a batter. Pour 1½ inches oil or lard into a deep fryer or heat in a deep pot on the stove. (Fat should be about 365°.) Coat shrimp thickly with batter and drop several shrimp at once into the hot fat. Cook until golden (3 to 4 minutes). Drain on absorbent towels. Allow fat to reheat some before frying more shrimp. (If you are using a deep fryer, put the basket in the fryer and then, with a spoon, lower the batter-coated shrimp into the hot fat so the shrimp won't stick to the bottom of the basket.) Serves 4.

CHAPTER FOUR

The Highlands and Valleys

TAXCO

*J*ALAPA, tucked in the hills of Veracruz, is often called "the garden city of Mexico" because it hosts so many flowers and fruits. The climate is temperate due to the altitude, but it borders on the tropics making the vegetation perennially lush. Jalapa is more often spelled "Xalapa" by its residents, but is always pronounced "Halapa."

The city is colonial in appearance with steep, winding streets, houses with tile roofs and long elegant windows that open to narrow balconies. We arrived late in the evening and headed for a downtown hotel. It was just before Christmas and driving through the melee was a bit like trying to negotiate a freeway during rush hour. In actuality, Jalapa is tranquil even though it is large (150,000 inhabitants) and the capital of the state. For some years it has been one of those Mexican hideaways that have attracted expatriates, not only because it's pretty in the traditional Spanish sense, but also because it has many cultural advantages. Jalapa houses the state university—a wooded, attractive campus (although a bit littered) where three Olmec heads sit at the entrance to the university's anthropological museum—and is well known for its symphony and dance company.

We were hungry that first night and found some delicious chicken enchiladas in a small café near the hotel. Like chicken soup, the chicken enchilada is a classic of Mexican cuisine, a simple dish that is at its best when prepared at the last minute. The secrets—tender, flavorful chicken, fresh homemade tortillas, and *crema.* The taste is not quite the same in this facsimile but is memorable enough.

ENCHILADAS DE POLLO

(Chicken Enchiladas)

1 small chicken, quartered or in pieces	1 dozen corn tortillas
1½ cups water	Finely shredded lettuce
Salt	Sliced radishes
½ cup *crema* (page 119)	Lime wedges

In a stew pot, put chicken and water, salt lightly and bring to a boil. Reduce heat and simmer until chicken is tender (about 1 hour). Pour off broth and refrigerate it until fat has set. Cool chicken, then skin and bone the meat and shred it finely.

TO MAKE ENCHILADAS: Skim fat off chicken broth and retain both. Heat shredded chicken with ½ cup of the broth and salt to taste. In a separate pan heat *crema* with ¼ cup broth and keep warm, but not boiling. On a griddle soften each tortilla by frying lightly in a little of the chicken fat. Then immediately dip the tortilla in the *crema* mixture, fill it with 2 tablespoons of shredded chicken and roll into a tube. Keep enchilada hot on a serving dish while repeating this process, for all the other tortillas. Pour remaining *crema* over enchiladas. Garnish with lettuce, sliced radishes, and lime wedges. Serves 4.

Leaving Jalapa we backtracked by Veracruz, dipping down and then upward toward Córdoba, beginning one of the most photographed routes in Mexico. A lot of history is packed into this part of the country. I couldn't help but think of the early treks from Veracruz to Mexico City that took days instead of hours, and even earlier when the transporting was done by Indian carriers exploited by wealthy Aztecs. These carriers were called *tamemes* and wore primitive versions of the backpack except that a front strap ran around their foreheads, causing, I should imagine, a continual headache. The conquering Spaniards had no more heart. Even after horses and mules were brought into New Spain, these carriers were still sent into the areas where the animals could not go. This head-braced system of transporting supplies continued for all types of expeditions in the Americas until the end of the nineteenth century. Today you will occasionally see a man carrying a load of wood or rocks *tameme*-style, but this time by his own choice.

We drove through the sugar cane area, to Córdoba where we stopped for a cup of coffee. All these highland towns are attractive. The buildings are brightly painted and the streets are clean and well maintained. This is mango area, and those beautiful big trees flanked by green cane fields lend a richness to the surrounding landscape.

Another twenty miles further on is Fortín de las Flores, one of the places recommended for the timid in tourist brochures. A town so serene and so abundantly flowered must appeal to

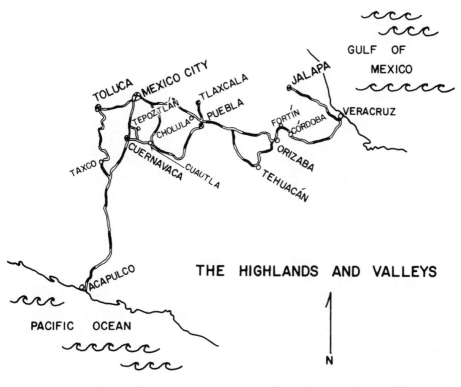

THE HIGHLANDS AND VALLEYS

The Highlands and Valleys 69

everyone. I know it's very popular with "weekenders" from the capital, which is easy to understand because in Mexico City these days it's sometimes difficult to breathe. Even as far south from the city limits as Puebla (1½ hours on the toll road) the air can be thick with industrial smoke. But Fortín is clear, and the great Orizaba volcano is visible from many windows. And if it is not, you can be sure the haze is heaven-sent, not man-made.

A fort built here by Cortés was called Fortress of the Flowers because the gardens have always produced a profusion of orchids, azaleas, camellias, gardenias, carnations, etc. It's as lovely as it sounds and a perfect place to try a chicken dish heavily influenced by nutmeg. *Pollo en Cebolla* (Chicken in Onions) is easy to duplicate because parsley can be substituted for the cilantro as nutmeg is the dominant flavor. Another version of this recipe is made with just a hatful of onions and no nutmeg. It might also be called *Pollo con Cebolla* (Chicken with Onions).

POLLO EN CEBOLLA
(Chicken in Onions)

1 medium chicken, quartered	with fine nutmeg or rind grater
3 tablespoons oil	1 teaspoon salt
2 medium onions, thinly sliced	1 teaspoon thyme
2 large cloves garlic, minced	2 tablespoons minced cilantro (or parsley)
1 whole nutmeg, grated	1 cup hot chicken broth
	⅓ cup medium-dry sherry

Wipe chicken with a damp cloth and dry. Heat oil in a heavy-bottomed stew pan, add chicken pieces and brown well. Remove chicken from pan and add onions and garlic to remaining oil. Stir and brown well over a low heat (about 20 minutes). Mix together nutmeg, salt, thyme, and cilantro and stir mixture into onions. Add hot broth and chicken, covering chicken parts with onion mixture. Cover tightly and simmer for about 1 hour. Add sherry and continue cooking another ½ hour or until chicken is very tender. Serve with *Arroz Verde* (page 120), or *Arroz a la Mexicana* (page 22). Serves 4.

We continued on through Orizaba, another flowered city, and quite an industrial complex. It is the home of two of Mexico's famous beers, *Dos XX* and *Superior*. If the traveler is curious about another of Mexico's bottled beverages, a swing down to Tehuacán is easy from here. Bottled mineral water, enjoying great popularity in this country, is also the savior of the tourist in Mexico whose not-unfounded fears of the tap water are calmed by labels like *Tehuacán* or *Peñefiel.* In the area around Tehuacán are the mineral springs from which the waters come and where they are bottled under strict standards. It's also a very popular resort area for people from the larger cities.

From Orizaba to Puebla on the toll road is only a short ride. If you start in the morning you may want to take a side trip into Tlaxcala, the smallest state in Mexico and a little northeast of Puebla. The country around the capital city (also called Tlaxcala) is hilly, lightly forested, and mostly Indian. The Tlaxcalans were second to the Tononacs in allying (albeit unwillingly) with Cortés to defeat the Aztecs. The state now is known for fine woolens, and some feel that the very best *sarapes* come from Santa Ana, a small village near the capital. I have been told that there are Indian markets where sellers still compute in old Spanish weights and measures. Even though the metric system was legally instituted into Mexico's education and trade at the end of the nineteenth century, a buyer in these parts might find herself having cloth measured in *vargas,* or have coins counted back to him in *reales.* This never happened to me, but the possibility was intriguing.

Puebla de los Angeles, "the town of the Angels," according to legend had been partly constructed by angels. They must have been Spanish angels because emotionally and architecturally the city is colonial—even today in its modernity. High, almost 7,000 feet, Puebla has a mild sunny climate and sometimes a clear view of the volcanoes, Popocatépetl and Ixtaccí-huatl. The urban smog that has had such a stranglehold on Mexico City for the past decade is now finding a base in Puebla. We talked to a Swiss businessman on our last visit who said that the influx of foreign residents and investments like his, and the general industrial growth (with the major Mexican Volkswagen plant located in Puebla) has doubled the city's population in the last ten years, and caused some of the problems.

Still, Puebla is remarkable clean and classy—and a busy stop for the energetic tourist. It is perhaps best known for its tile and pottery, a result of the influence of the Talavara potters from Spain. Although the Talavara color glazes are beautiful, I think the Puebla tile is much livelier. It's the Indian touch—the passion for painting figures, flowers, and animals on craft items.

The traditional dress of Puebla is called the *china poblana* and there is an interesting story of its origin. Early in the nineteenth century a young woman of Asian or East Indian extraction was captured by pirates and somehow ended up in Mexico—in Veracruz, where a kindly gentleman from Puebla took her home to his childless wife. They raised her as their daughter and she became a kind and gracious woman who, in gratitude, devoted her life to charity. She had adopted a style of dress which she always wore—a skirt of red wool bordered with green, and a white embroidered blouse. Over the years the costume has become a bit more garish with spangles and such and is now usually worn only as fiesta attire. The *Poblana* of today is chic, contemporary, and decidedly urban in her dress.

As far as culinary accomplishments are concerned, Puebla cannot be overlooked. One of the most famous dishes in all of the republic, comes from this city. *Mole Poblano de Guajolote* (Puebla Mole with Turkey) is a dish said to have originated at the Convent of Santa Rosa where the nuns, wishing to thank the visiting archbishop for funding a new wing of their building, concocted a stew with almost every food from the kitchen. Loosely translated, *mole* means a stewy sauce, a multi-ingredient mixture, but most first-timers in Mexico think of it as the sauce that contains both *chiles* and chocolate. This is true with some *moles* (the *Puebla Mole*, for example), but it is more accurate to say that *mole* tastes like nothing you have ever had before. I think it is delicious!

MOLE POBLANO CON GUAJOLOTE
(Puebla Mole with Turkey)

10 *chiles mulatos*
9 *chiles pasillas*
7 *chiles anchos*
⅓ cup lard
12 pound turkey, quartered
8 tablespoons lard
½ cup sesame seeds
¼ teaspoon anise seed
6 coriander seeds
10 peppercorns
4 whole cloves
6 small, green tomatoes, cooked or canned

1 large onion, chopped
¼ cup raisins
3 tablespoons unshelled pumpkin seeds
½ cup almonds
¼ cup skinless peanuts
1 corn tortilla
1½ cups chicken broth
⅓ cup lard
2 ounces bitter-sweet chocolate
Salt

The night before serving this dish, core, seed, and devein chiles. Fry chiles in lard (a little lard, a few chiles at a time) very briefly. They should not brown. Put in a large bowl, cover with water, and let soak overnight. In the morning drain off water and purée chiles in blender.

For the rest of the recipe, allow about five hours before serving in order to cook turkey and prepare *mole*. First, brown turkey quarters each in 2 tablespoons lard. Transfer browned pieces to a large pan and steam above water until tender (about 3 hours). (I use my canning pan and reverse the canning rack to act as a steamer.) Cool slightly and remove meat from bones.

Meanwhile, toast sesame seeds, anise seed, and coriander in a hot ungreased skillet for several minutes. In a spice grinder or with a mortar and pestle grind toasted spices with peppercorns and cloves and combine in blender with green tomatoes and onions. Toast raisins in ungreased skillet for several minutes, followed by pumpkin seeds (which pop so keep a lid handy). Add these ingredients to blender along with almonds, peanuts, and a lightly toasted, stale tortilla. Add enough chicken broth to make a smooth paste.

Cook prepared chile purée in hot lard (this tends to fly around when hot so be careful) for 8 to 10 minutes and then add blender ingredients. Melt chocolate in double boiler and add to mixture with salt to taste. Add turkey pieces to heat through and serve with *Arroz Blanco* (page 37). Serves 12. If you have a smaller group this dish freezes well for later use—in fact, the flavors improve.

Puebla is also known for its confections. All lovers of sweets will have a field day in the candy shops with their exquisite and indescribable creations. A common sweet-potato candy found in the booths and stores of Puebla has its story, too, one very touching and pious.

Many years ago, a lovely young girl from a farm in Querétaro chose to enter a convent, much against her parents' desires for she was their only child, a sweet girl, and a very fine cook. Still she was insistent and entered the novitiate in Puebla while her parents continued to entreat her not to take the final vows. Finally, her father sent her some of their sweet potatoes, saying he was hungry for them and asking her to prepare them as she had at home. He thought it might persuade her to return. She answered quickly, asking her parents to come to Puebla as she wanted to see them. It took them a while to get there in those days, and when they arrived there was a note from their daughter saying that her last act before receiving her veil had been to make the candies for her father, and that she was including the directions. In time, she became a saint—Santa Clara, and the candies are known as *Los Comotes de Santa Clara* (Sweet Potatoes of Saint Clara). I love the story, but not the candy, I'm sorry to say.

I do like the almond *ate* (paste) dish which I tried in Puebla. This is known as *Postre de Almendra* which literally translates to dessert of almonds. It's sweet, but I love an almond taste, it is easy to duplicate and will be very well received by dessert lovers.

POSTRE DE ALMENDRA

(Almond Dessert)

2 cups sugar
1 cup water
2 cinnamon sticks
⅓ cup medium-dry
    sherry
1½ cups shelled almonds
6 large egg yolks,
    lightly beaten

1 pound sponge or
    pound cake, thinly
    sliced
Crema (page 119) or sour
    cream

Combine sugar, water, and cinnamon sticks and boil for 5 to 6 minutes. Discard cinnamon sticks and pour ½ of the sugar mixture into a shallow bowl and mix with sherry. Grind almonds fine in a blender and combine with remaining sugar mixture and beaten yolks. Cook over a low heat until hot and thickened. Dip cake slices in sherry syrup and line the bottom of a 1-quart baking dish. Cover cake layer with almond paste and repeat until you have 3 layers of cake and 3 layers of almond paste. Bake, uncovered, in a 350° oven for 15 to 20 minutes or until top is lightly browned. Serve hot or cold with a dollop or *crema* or sour cream. Serves 6.

Also from Puebla are the little stuffed appetizers called *Chalupas de Puebla* (Fried Tortillas, Puebla-style). The dough is the same as for *Sopes* except these are shaped like boats instead of little pie shells. In Puebla the dough is filled with pork and green chile sauce. Follow the recipe for making the *Sopes* shells (page 95), and shape them like little dinghies. Then fill them with *Puerco con Chile Verde* (page 99), and top them with a dollop of *crema* (page 119).

There is so much to see in Puebla that a traveler could return again and again. It is a very Catholic city with elaborate churches and a rich regional museum. The stately library in the city hall houses some 50,000 old volumes, ancient maps, and chronicles for the scholar of Hispanic studies.

In my fascination with Mexican city planning I was amused—no impressed—to discover that the streets running north to south are called just that, *calles* (streets). They are numbered, with the even in the eastern section of the city and the odd in the western part. The streets running east and west are called *avenidas* (avenues), and the even-numbered ones are in the north and the odd are in the south. It's very easy to get around in Puebla—it's the parking that's frustrating.

Another tale of Catholic Puebla concerns the history of the Secret Convent of Santa Mónica. This was one of the earliest convents founded in New Spain, but it was closed in 1857 when all the convents in Mexico were forbidden by the government to operate. Nearly a century later, in 1934, the police in Puebla were made aware that large quantities of food were going into a house across the street from—of all places—the police station. The house was checked as was the entire block of buildings which, in Mexican cities and towns, connect with common walls. Nothing unusual was revealed then except that a portion of the block was unaccounted for by the city engineers and no one seemed to be able to trace ownership of the space.

Finally, a persistent detective noticed a light flashing on the wall in the dining room of the house under suspicion. A button was located and with one solid push the wall moved and the authorities found themselves facing a nun with a food order for the day. An extensive search led to the discovery of a small, but complete, convent with sixteen elderly nuns in residence. Since there were beds for more, it was assumed the younger, more agile sisters had vaulted into hiding elsewhere. The convent had two inner patios and an arrangement whereby the nuns were able to stand and hear mass in the corner of the Church of Santa Mónica without being seen by the parishioners. In time, other convents were uncovered in Puebla and ultimately the trappings of convent life in Puebla were all transferred to Santa Mónica which is open to the public. Such stories of piety and dedication always surprise me but they are so Mexican.

From Puebla we were off to Cuernavaca by way of nearby Cholula, once a major pre-Columbian center. Originally built by the Toltecs, Cholula became a ceremonial city dedicated to Quetzalcoatl. The legend of this figure is the most retold in Mexico. In short, Quetzalcoatl was the son of a Toltec chief, although he was said to be divinely conceived as a result of his mother swallowing a piece of jade. As a boy he was strong, brave, and wise, and was set out to reform the Toltec empire. After a time, the priests grew tired of his good intentions and successes and tricked him into breaking his vow of chastity. He disappeared from the area in shame, saying he would return someday. (Apparently he resurfaced in the Yucatán where a similar figure appears later in the Mayan religion.) The name Quetzalcoatl means "plumed serpent." Coming from Nahuatl, the main, original Indian language, in which *quetzal* means feathered and *coatl* is serpent. Quetzal is also the name of the sacred bird of the Mayas and a monetary unit of Guatemala, so there are many spin-offs from this legend. The one that altered the course of history in the Americas is that Cortés was mistaken at first for the returning Quetzalcoatl. Certainly this improved his chances in his conquest of the Aztecs.

Cholula is rife with pyramids. The main one, in honor of Quetzalcoatl, has one of the largest bases in the world. However, Cortés, in his anger over a Cholulan plot to kill him, ordered all of the temples (basically pyramids) torn down and replaced with Catholic churches. Apparently it is not easy to lay waste to a pyramid. The command was sloppily executed and Cholula is now a city of churches on top of ruins. The pyramid to Quetzalcoatl supports *Nuestra Señora de los Remedios* (Our Lady of Remedies), an impressive tiled and domed church that can be seen for miles. It looks as though the church is sitting on a hill, but the "hill" is a pyramid underneath the church that is now under excavation. I cannot imagine a more curious mixture of architecture after the work is completed.

Cuernavaca, from Mexico City, is a short drive on the toll road, making it a possible commute and certainly a weekend and summer vacation spot. It's easy to get to Cuernavaca from anywhere in the highlands and I think it is one of the most climatically desirable places in Mexico. It's the capital of the state of Morelos, 5,000 feet high with year-round balmy air, and flowers in abundance. It was in Cuernavaca in the early nineteenth century that Joel Poinsett, the American minister to Mexico, discovered the beautiful red Christmas flower. He took it back to the United States where it was popularized as the "Poinsettia."

Cuernavaca has a history of popularity. The Aztec emperors loved it. Cortés chose it for his personal retirement spot (after establishing the sugar cane fields that now surround the city). His palace is downtown, and now a state musuem. José de la Borda, the silver magnate of Taxco in the early eighteenth century, built a beautiful home and garden for his priest son. It later became the summer palace for the beleaguered Emperor Maximilian and his wife, Carlota. She, a great romantic, especially loved the Borda gardens which still remain.

Cuernavaca has had its struggles, too. The Spanish *hacendado* wealth attracted reformists and revolution in the early part of this century when the idealistic Indian leader Emiliano Zapata and his followers, reflecting the deep frustration of the peasants, razed the surrounding sugar plantations. Between the loyalist troops and the Zapatistas, Cuernavaca and its residents suffered more destruction and hunger than any other area in Mexico at that time.

However, none of this strife is visible today. The town is busy, clean, touristic, residential, and attractive on all levels. Wandering along the streets on my first visit I sampled *Carnitas* from a little lunch counter that opened onto the sidewalk. These tacos have a shredded, browned pork filling and when eating them, I realized the difference between Mexican tacos and the type that originated in the southwestern United States.

Meat is the only filling for the *auténtico* and it is topped only with a little *salsa*—not cheese, tomatoes, lettuce, etc. The tortillas are warm, but soft—not fried. Such is the real stuff.

CARNITAS
(Little Meats)

1 4 to 4½ pound pork butt or shoulder	Salt
Water	Warm, corn tortillas (page 131)*
1 teaspoon each oregano and ground cumin	*Salsa Cruda* (page 13) or *Salsa Verde* (page 79)
1 large onion, sliced	

Put pork in a pot with water to cover and add oregano, cumin, and onion. Bring to a boil, cover and simmer until tender (2 to 3 hours). Remove meat from pot and transfer to an oven dish. (Cooking water can be saved for stock.) Salt well and place in a 350° oven for about 1 hour or until pork is well browned. Pour off fat and shred or chop meat into small pieces. Serve warm in warm tortillas with *salsa*. Serves 8 to 10.

*These make good appetizers in small tortillas—the size made for *Sopes* (page 95). If you are using commercial tortillas, just cut a smaller circle in the tortilla and save the outer ring for *Rajas de Pollo* (page 139), or *Sopa de Lima* (page 53). (These scraps can also be frozen for later use.)

SALSA VERDE
(Green Sauce)

1 10- or 13-ounce can of tomatillos (Mexican green tomatoes), drained	½ cup chopped cilantro
	2 canned *chiles jalapeños* or *serranos,* chopped
2 cloves garlic, mashed	Salt to taste

Put all ingredients, except salt, in blender and blend until smooth. Salt to taste. *Salsa* can be heated in a small saucepan or served cold over *Carnitas* (page 79).

One of Cuernavaca's interesting side trips is to the higher valley of Tepoztlán, supposedly the birthplace of Quetzalcoatl. Certainly it has remained quaintly Indian. In fact, Nahuatl was still widely spoken here well into this century. Tepoztlán has a pyramid in the mountains high above the town. It's not always visible, but it's comforting to the tourist that above is a shrine dedicated to the God of *pulque*. Where else could you enjoy a glass of spirits more than in Tepoztlán?

Closer to Cuernavaca is the town of Cuautla where we stopped to have lunch and look for *huaraches*. My brother and I are *huarache* lovers and tend to head first for the sandal and leather sections of Mexican markets. I'm always reminded of reading D. H. Lawrence's essay on "Market Day" in his book, *Morning in Mexico:*

The natives use human excrement for tanning leather. When Bernal Diaz came with Cortés to the great market place of Mexico City, in Montezuma's day, he saw little pots of human excrement in rows for sale, and the leather-makers going around sniffing to see which was the best, before they paid for it. It staggered even a 15th-century Spaniard. Yet my leather man and myself think it screamingly funny that I smell the huaraches before buying them. Everything has its own smell, and the natural smell of huaraches is what it is. You might as well quarrel with an onion for smelling like an onion.

I think *huaraches* smell like leather, but it is a specific Mexican leather smell. However, I would hesitate to pick up a sandal and smell it seriously in case the vendor had some notion of past customs.

Cuautla is the hometown of Zapata and full of strong Indian faces. There is an odd density about it. The air was hot and heavy when we were there, even though it was winter, and the town was thick with people and traffic. It also brims with foliage all year around—flowers, fruit trees, broad-leafed tropical plants, and trailing vines—and obviously is a pleasant place to live because it is centered around mineral springs and there are private resorts as well as pools that are open to the public.

In spite of the hot weather, we ordered soup, which was delicious and worth any trouble in getting the recipe. *Sopa de*

Calabaza could mean any kind of squash soup, but in this case it's zucchini, a prolific plant that seems appropriate to the heavy vegetation of Cuautla. Also popular in Mexico is a soup made from the blossom of the squash plant, *Sopa de Flor de Calabaza.* Anyone who has squash plants in a garden can afford this recipe as it is a way to use the prolific male blossom. (Save a few for fertilizing the female blossom.) The male squash blossom does not produce a squash and has a straight stem, whereas the female blossom has a little bulge at the base of the blossom. I think a soup made of blossoms is very exotic.

SOPA DE CALABAZA
(Squash Soup)

1 pound zucchini or any summer squash, chopped	Salt, pepper, oregano
	1 egg yolk
	½ cup light cream (half-and-half)
1 large onion, chopped	
6 cups chicken stock	Lime wedges

Simmer squash and onions in stock until tender, then blend until smooth. Season to taste with salt, pepper, and oregano. Beat egg yolk with cream and add a small amount of hot squash liquid to it, beating as you add. Continue to add small amounts of hot soup to the egg mixture until you have about 2 cups of liquid. Add this very slowly to the rest of the hot, not boiling, soup to prevent curdling. Serve with lime wedges and hot *bolillos.* Serves 4.

SOPA DE FLOR DE CALABAZA
(Squash Blossom Soup)

3 dozen mature male squash blossoms	2 egg yolks
1 cup minced onion	1 cup light cream (half-and-half)
3 tablespoons butter	Salt
6 cups rich chicken broth	Pepper

Remove stems from squash blossoms and chop blossoms coarsely. Sauté onions in butter in a soup pot. When onions are soft, stir in squash blossoms and add chicken stock. Cover and simmer ten minutes. Beat egg yolks with cream and stir in slowly just before serving. (Soup should not be boiling.) Salt and pepper to taste. Serves 4 to 6.

Once you get off the toll road from Cuernavaca, the route to Taxco is winding and interesting and sometimes, depending on the season, misty and a bit hair-raising. I love the hills which flower even during the winter. In the summer they are green, and, as you go around the final curves of the road toward the city, the hills are stepped with red and white houses.

Taxco is one of the prettiest towns in Mexico, the one you envision when you plan your first trip to the country. Built on hillsides and in little ravines (over the mines), Taxco's streets are cobbled and narrow as ribbons. Unless you have a small car and are a seasoned driver of skinny streets, it's best to walk around Taxco or take a taxi. More than once I have been stuck going up a street that narrows like a pencil point, hemmed in by four or five trucks going up or down while leaning on their horns. Admidst all this confusion, streams of people walk in and out of the stalled traffic. Such situations have been known to make even the most patient driver hate Taxco after the first trip and refuse ever to go back.

The little city is beautiful, though. The houses are built almost on top of each other and the streets and plazas vibrate with life all day and through much of the night. It is so picturesque that the government of Mexico has voted it a national monument and all new buildings must be built in the same colonial style.

The silver history of Taxco began with the Aztecs who had discovered both gold and silver in the Guerrero hills. It was Cortés and his passion for precious metals that put Taxco on the map. In the early eighteenth century two French brothers, the de la Bordas, made the silver mining in Taxco into a real operation. Until the end of the century the mines continued to produce. So much silver came out of Mexico and Peru between the late sixteenth century and the early nineteenth century that the two countries minted close to two billion dollars in silver (in a day when a dollar had the value of fifty), and about that much silver again was sent to Spain to be minted there. These figures, of course, include all of the silver mines in Mexico.

But Taxco's silver boom ended after José de la Borda died. Not until the early 1930s did the silver industry revive again. An American professor of architecture, William Spratling, began to make silver items from the local ore. In time he taught local craftsmen to do the same and Taxco became the "Silver City" of Mexico. Today it is a bustling tourist town with good accommodations and more gold and silver items than you'd ever hope to see.

The center plaza in Taxco is surrounded by shops and hotels, and, notably, the beautiful Santa Prisca Church built by the very pious José de la Borda. Crowds of *chamacos* (street kids, acting as guides, who hustle pesos) swarm around, offering to help choose your shop. But it's easy to find your own shopping places since there are literally dozens of little stores on the plaza and tucked in the narrow alleys under balconies covered with potted flowers.

The food is good, too. We had a delicious version of *Pollo Borracho* (Drunken Chicken) in Taxco. Drunken sauces made with pulque are common on barbecued meats and chicken, but this is cooked in the oven with tequila and *chorizo,* the Mexican spiced sausage. It was served with *Arroz Blanco* (page 37).

POLLO BORRACHO
(Drunken Chicken)

4 tablespoons oil	1½ cup orange juice
2 *chiles pasillas*	½ cup white tequilla
1 medium onion, chopped	6 tablespoons oil or lard
1½ cup bulk *chorizo* (page 85)	1½ chickens cut in quarters (6 pieces)

Heat oil in frying pan. Core and seed chiles, break into pieces and fry lightly in oil. Remove chiles from pan with slotted

spoon and transfer to blender. Add onions to remaining oil and
sauté until softened. Add *chorizo* and continue to cook over a
low heat until *chorizo* is cooked through (about 8 to 10 minutes).
Add orange juice to blender and blend chiles smooth. Add to
chorizo mixture along with tequila. Stir to heat through and keep
warm while browning chicken.

Heat 3 tablespoons of oil or lard and brown 2 pieces of
chicken at a time, adding more oil or lard as necessary. Transfer
browned chicken to a baking dish and when all the chicken is
browned, pour the *borracho* sauce over it. Bake, covered, in a
325° oven for about 1½ hours or until chicken is very tender.
Serve with *Arroz Blanco* (page 37). Serves 6.

The road from Taxco to Toluca (or vice versa) winds some,
but it's good road, scenic, not heavily traveled, and a splendid,
easy way to avoid Mexico City. It's also another marvel in road
engineering. Here in the central section of Mexico, the earth
seems to be going in every direction, and each state is a natural
barrier to the next—the epitome of geologic planlessness.
Closer to Toluca the *barrancas* on either side of the road form
giant gashes, cutting off side access for miles, and the ground
around Toluca is so barren and geometrically eroded that much
of it looks like the ruins of an ancient civilization.

There are a couple of stops worth noting on this road. Ixtapán
de la Sal is a pretty, well-kept mineral spa, popular with people
from the capital. The government owns and operates the springs
and there are good public facilities for local people and tourists
alike. The buildings in the town are whitewashed with brightly
painted stripes of color on the bottom.

Just before Toluca is the pottery town of Metepec off to the
right. Ceramics are an old tradition in this village, and some
wonderful color glazes are used.

Toluca is the highest city in Mexico, almost 9,000 feet. On
entering, the moonscape-like area surrounding the city and the
strange, blank mountain behind it give a desolate look to this
capital city of the State of Mexico. However, once inside, Toluca
seems more friendly. The downtown municipal and capital

buildings are old Spanish and the market is one of the best in Mexico, especially on Friday. It's known for wool blankets, *sarapes* and sweaters, and a huge selection of baskets. Toluca is popular with tourists (and pickpockets, so watch your *pesos*). In this big market the venders really like to bargain. I have trouble bartering but can get in the swing of it in Toluca— shrugging, grimacing, or waving my forefinger emphatically in the typical Mexican gesture that means, "No deal, José." Then just as I walk off in mock disgust, I am lured back with another compromise—of course not without a woeful accusation that I am taking tortillas out of the mouths of children.

Toluca does have its regional specialty, although it's impossible to duplicate it exactly because the pork is so good in that region. *Chorizo,* Mexico's seasoned pork sausage, is the base for many dishes and is as important in the Mexican kitchen as ground beef is in American cooking. The idea of the sausage first came from Spain where it is usually smoked, but in Mexico the pork is stuffed fresh into the casings or stored in bulk. Both versions are duplicated in the western United States, but I find the cased sausage spoils easily (usually in the store) and the bulk *chorizo* tends to spread out in the pan, stewing and foaming, so that I'm never sure if it has been fully cooked. The following recipe is quite easy if you have a meat grinder (in Mexico they often chop it fine), and the spoilage problem is solved by freezing it in small packages for use when needed. Freeze it for several days to season.

CHORIZO DE TOLUCA
(Toluca Pork Sausage)

3 *chiles anchos*	5 whole cloves
2 *chiles pasillas*	½ teaspoon cumin seed
¼ cup tequila	1 teaspoon oregano
½ cup water	4 cloves garlic, minced
2½ pounds boneless lean pork (but with fat rind)	3 tablespoons sweet paprika
1 teaspoon coriander seeds	2½ teaspoons salt
	½ teaspoon cinnamon
	½ cup vinegar

The night before, toast the *chiles* lightly over a burner flame or in an ungreased skillet. (Do not brown.) Core and seed them and break them into pieces. Pour tequila and water over chiles and let sit overnight. In the morning, grind the meat (or have it previously ground by the butcher) and transfer to a large bowl. Purée *chile* mixture and add to pork. In a spice grinder or with a mortar and pestle grind coriander, cloves, and cumin, and add to pork with the remaining ingredients. Mix well and freeze in ¼ pound packages. Makes 10 packages.

CHAPTER FIVE

The South

OAXACA

$\mathcal{T}$HE Pan-American Highway from the highlands to Oaxaca is arduous but spectacular and a strong tribute to Mexican engineering. Oaxaca is less than 350 miles from Mexico City, yet it is a full day's drive, and although there are daily plane flights that connect the two cities, the drive through the Sierra Madre del Sur is well worth the time and energy. When I drove into the Valley of Oaxaca for the first time, I felt I had entered another time zone, a new culture, a completely different geography. It was all of that!

It's a good climb leaving the state of Puebla, and before long the mountains with their scrub foilage seem to stretch endlessly ahead. The pottery lover may find a brief intermission in Acatlán a few hours down the road. This town is known for its cheerfully painted clay sculptures of animals, birds, and people, all pyramided into tree shapes—popular items with tourists. Farther on the gray-green maguey plantations become visible. Maguey grows happily in this rugged terrain and provides a nice contrast to the somber ochres and browns of the surrounding hills. Mescal, a popular drink in Oaxaca, is a fermented liquor made from the heart of this agave variety and is bottled with the worm of the plant—a horrifying little extra to most newcomers.

A little more should be said here about the agave succulent whose species not only produce the fibers we know as sisal (*henequén* or hemp) mentioned in the chapter on the Yucatán, but also are the sources for three popular liquors in Mexico— mescal, pulque, and tequila. Also in the same family is a plant whose tubercles, called peyote, are considered hallucinogenic and are fundamental to the religious ceremonies of the northern Mexican Indians, the Yaquis and the Huichols. The agave also claims kin to the century plant of the southwestern United States.

The Aztecs were the first to extract and ferment pulque, and it's still a common drink in Mexico. (Tourists love to count the the number of *pulquerías*—small bars—in any given town.) It's the chief cheap drink of the country, although in my estimation it's pretty awful. However, it does add flavor to meat sauces. Once, many years ago when my son Lee was small, we stopped for *comida* in the beautiful Virrey Mendoza Hotel in Morelia. The dining room at that time had stately, dark-paneled rooms with colonial furniture and snowy table linens. Exquisitely tender slices of pork loin fixed in a pulque sauce were served and Lee, a reluctant eater at best, loved the meal and ate his entire portion, remarking for miles after how good that "pork and pulque" tasted. Some years later he flew to Washington on a dinner flight and when I talked to him the next day, I asked what he had had to eat.

"Oh," he said. "It was terrific! It was pork and pulque."

I was impressed that he had remembered, but I suspect on that domestic airline it was probably beef and gravy.

Tequila is surely the best drink from the agave cactus. It is extracted from the heart of the smaller, bluish plant that is grown extensively in the plateau and lake regions of Mexico. It is named after the town in the state of Jalisco where the distillation process originated, and ranges in color from clear to amber in the more aged varieties. The clear tequila is used for mixed drinks while the gold varieties are sipped neat from small glasses, staggered with a lick of salt and a bit of lime.

Back on the Oaxaca road, we curve and wind for another fifty miles to the Valley of Yanhuitlán. Here is the convent and church of Santo Domingo de Yanhuitlán, a lone monument to the silent countryside, but worth a visit into the chapel. Built in the seventeenth century by Dominican missionaries (and thousands of Indians) the interior of this church contains paintings and an elegantly sculptured altar that date back to the time of the original construction. After leaving Yanhuitlán the road climbs quickly to 8,000 feet. This area has no flat plains, but little *milpas* (cornfields) hug the hillsides as the road descends into the Valley of Oaxaca, a high plateau of 5,000 feet, ringed with hills and mountains.

Oaxaca is an adaptation of a Zapotec Indian name—something like Uaxayac—a toss-up in pronounciation. The city is lovely with old colonial homes and lots of jacaranda trees. It is laid out more or less in a grid, which makes it easy to follow maps but also easy to get lost, since Mexican streets have such marked similarities. I remember once wandering around for hours, looking for our car and thinking all the while that it was "just over there a couple of streets, parked by an auto-parts store"— one of a dozen or so auto-parts stores in that area.

The *zócalo* or main plaza is the center of activity and a good pivotal point from which to explore Oaxaca. The trees and fountains are pretty and it's nice to sit under the portals around the plaza and watch the goings-on. Although the state of Oaxaca claims at least two dozen different Indian tribes, Mixtec and Zapotec are the most predominant in and around the capital city. Their languages are heard as commonly as Spanish. In the middle of the plaza, we found tiny Indian women weaving vibrantly colored *rebozos* on small hand looms that hook on one end over the back part of benches and are tied at the other around the women's waists. They worked and chattered while their children, dressed in exquisitely embroidered *huipals* and nothing else, scampered around their mothers.

There is a lot to see in Oaxaca. The churches are perhaps the finest and best preserved in Mexico. The Basílica de la Soledad, built of carved stone, houses La Virgen de la Soledad (The Virgin of Solitude), the patron saint of Oaxaca. She is a beautifully crafted statue and greatly valued by Oaxaqueños. The Church of Santo Domingo, not impressive on the outside, is something else in its interior. Another Dominican creation from the sixteenth century, it contains a fortune in gold leaf, polychrome sculpture, paving-tile floors, gold chandeliers, and large oil paintings—baroque beyond belief!

Next to the church is the Regional Museum of Oaxaca, a favorite of mine. Built around an open courtyard (the building was originally a convent attached to the Church of Santo Domingo), the museum features life-size figures depicting the

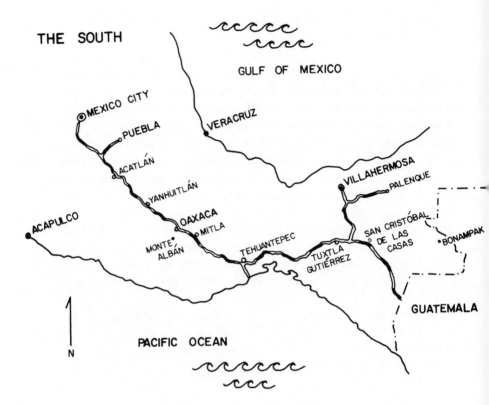

THE SOUTH

GULF OF MEXICO

MEXICO CITY
PUEBLA
VERACRUZ
ACATLÁN
YANHUITLÁN
VILLAHERMOSA
PALENQUE
ACAPULCO
OAXACA
MITLA
MONTE ALBÁN
TEHUANTEPEC
SAN CRISTÓBAL DE LAS CASAS
BONAMPAK
TUXTLA GUTIÉRREZ
GUATEMALA
PACIFIC OCEAN
N

lifestyles, crafts, and costumes of the different Indian groups
of the area. It also contains the incredible Monte Albán jewels—
thought to be the greatest treasure find in the Americas.

To me, Oaxaca's greatest treasure is a recipe for the delicious
Sopa de Frijol Negro (Black Bean Soup). As mentioned in the
chapter on the Yucatán, black beans are native to southern
Mexico, and especially popular in Oaxaca. For that matter
Oaxaqueños do well with any type bean. This may be because
of the predominance of Indians in the area, but whatever the
explanation, beans are synonomous with Oaxaca. In fact, the
first black beans I found in Califronia were shipped from the
Oaxaca region.

FRIJOLES

(Beans)

Use dried black, pinto pink, or Mexican red beans for this recipe. (Do not use kidney beans as they get too mushy.)

1. Rinse and pick over beans. Put 2 cups of beans in a large pot with 6 cups of water. (1 to 3 is the general ratio of beans to liquid.) Soak overnight if desired, but use the same water for cooking.
2. Bring water to a boil, reduce heat and simmer, covered, for 1 hour.
3. Add 1 medium onion, chopped; 2 to 3 garlic cloves, mashed; and a small hamhock or 2 or 3 pieces of diced bacon or a little salt pork. Simmer, covered, until beans are tender (about 1½ to 2 hours). Add salt* to taste. Serves 4 to 5.

*Do not salt beans until their skins burst as they will toughen with salt.

REFRITOS

(Refried Beans)

These are not actually refried, but fried only once. They are called *refritos* in the Mexican tradition of redundancy for emphasis.

1. Drain cooked beans of any excess liquid, but retain it.
2. Heat 3 to 4 tablespoons corn, safflower, or peanut oil, or lard and fry 4 to 5 cups of beans over a medium heat. Mash well with a potato masher as you fry them and add a little of the bean liquid if they get too dry.

Use in, or serve with, any recipe calling for refried or fried beans. Serves 4 to 5.

SOPA DE FRIJOL NEGRO

(Black Bean Soup)

2 cups dried black beans
2 quarts water
1 large onion, finely
  chopped
3 cloves garlic, minced
½ pound meaty pork
  bone (loin, butt or
  fresh shank)
1 teaspoon oregano

½ cup tomato paste
Salt to taste
Thinly-sliced radishes
Finely-shredded cabbage
Minced *chiles serranos*
Crema (page 119) or
  commercial sour cream
Lime wedges

Rinse and pick over beans. Combine beans in a large pot with water and bring to a boil. Reduce heat, cover, and simmer for 1½ hours, then add onions, garlic, pork bone, and oregano. Cover and simmer for another 1½ to 2 hours until beans and pork are tender. Add tomato paste and salt to taste. Serve soup with separate bowls of radishes, cabbage, chiles, *crema,* and lime wedges for garnish. Serves 4 to 6.

NOTE: This is a thick soup, but add more water if too much liquid cooks away or a thinner consistency is desired.

Another Mexican specialty that we tried first in Oaxaca is the popular *antojito* (appetizer) called *sopes.* These are little tortilla shells filled with various savories—beans, potatoes, or bits of meat or sausage, and garnished with slightly vinegared lettuce, cabbage, radishes, and onions, and often topped with *crema.* In Oaxaca we had them with beans and potatoes and they were delightful.

SOPES

(Filled Tortilla Appetizer)

FILLING:

3 cups fried black beans
(page 93)
2 cups diced cooked
potatoes
1 small onion, quartered
and thinly sliced

3 tablespoons olive oil
2 tablespoons white or
red wine vinegar
Salt and pepper

SOPES:

1 recipe for tortilla dough
(page 131)

Oil for cooking

GARNISH:
Chopped fresh cilantro

Crema (page 119) or
commercial sour cream

Heat beans and keep warm. Toss potatoes and onions in olive oil and vinegar, salt and pepper to taste, and set aside.

Make tortilla dough and divide it into 12 2-inch balls. (You will have extras for experimenting.) Follow directions for pressing tortillas—making these for *sopes* about 3½ to 4 inches in diameter. Oil the griddle sparingly and cook one side of the tortilla very lightly (according to basic recipe). Turn over tortilla and cook on the other side, but as it is cooking pinch up the sides forming a lip like a little pie shell. Put a drop of oil in the middle of the shell as it is cooking and make sure the *sope* is cooked through before removing it. Keep cooked *sopes* warm until all are cooked. Fill each shell with about ½ cup of warm beans, topped with ¼ to ⅓ cup of potato and onion mixture. Sprinkle with cilantro and add a dollop of *crema* or sour cream. Serve as an appetizer or for a first course. Makes 12 *sopes*.

When in the Oaxaca area the traveler must visit the ruins of Monte Albán and Mitla, both easy day-excursions from the city. Mitla predates Monte Albán, but the latter is usually the first side trip since it is only a little over five miles from the center of the city. Built 2,000 years ago by the Zapotecs, Monte Albán was a holy city and supported many thousands of people in its prime. It is located on a high plateau, and from the edges a strong eye can identify many excavations below, showing where the city once extended. Although spectacular in craft and carving, it is a somber ruin for my taste, perhaps because when the Mixtecs conquered the Zapotecs they turned Monte Albán into a burial place, a shrine to the dead. However, the Mixtecs were master craftsmen and responsible for the beautiful gold objects and turquoise, jade, and ivory jewelry that were discovered in one of the tombs a few years ago. As I mentioned, these works are on display in the Regional Museum of Oaxaca.

Again, the size of the structures at Monte Albán and the great distances between steps makes one think these early Indians were of some large physical stature. However, they were tiny, not only by our standards but even by comparison to early Romans and Egyptians. (The average Roman soldier was 5 feet, 2 inches tall.) The small, but big-hearted and far-sighted, Benito Juárez, a nineteenth century president of Mexico, was a Zapotec Indian. And the short but despotic dictator for thirty-five years, Porfirio Díaz, was a Mixtec. Both men were from Oaxaca, but, understandably, Juárez gets all the local press.

Mitla, twenty-five miles south of Oaxaca, is an earlier construction by the Zapotecs, which was later also taken over by the Mixtecs. In fact, it was inhabited until the seventeenth century. It, too, was a ceremonial location but the architecture is quite different from Monte Albán. Many small stones carved in geometric patterns are imbedded in the walls of the building, and the impression is rather Grecian or Turkish—even a bit Chinese. It is a unique place, unlike Monte Albán or any of the many smaller ruins in the area.

Back in Oaxaca, we had a farewell breakfast of *Huevos Rancheros* (Ranch-style Eggs) before heading south to Tehuantepec. This is one of the standard dishes of Mexico having a number of variations, but it is most commonly made with a softly fried tortilla and fried eggs topped with a cooked tomato sauce. In Oaxaca they add a sprig of *epazote* to the sauce and a little *queso fresco* (crumbled fresh white cheese). A fair equivalent for this cheese would be a dry Farmers cheese, although *queso fresco* is available in many Mexican and Latin American grocery stores. The nice feature of *Huevos Rancheros* is that they are good for breakfast, brunch, lunch, or for a light supper. The ingredients are not difficult to find and almost everyone who likes eggs and Mexico likes this dish.

HUEVOS RANCHEROS
(Ranch-style Eggs)

SALSA:

1 medium onion, finely chopped
3 tablespoons safflower, corn, or peanut oil
3 large tomatoes, peeled, cored and chopped (or an equivalent amount of Italian or Mexican plum tomatoes)

1 to 2 cored and seeded *chiles serranos* (or 1 *jalapeño*), minced
2 tablespoons minced cilantro
1 sprig of *epazote*
Salt and pepper

Oil
8 eggs
8 corn tortillas

1 cup crumbled dry white cheese (*queso fresco*)

In a heavy-bottomed saucepan sauté onions in oil. Then add tomatoes, chiles, cilantro, and *epazote*. Cover and simmer until tomatoes are cooked and blended, then salt and pepper to taste. Keep warm while preparing tortillas and eggs.

Heat oil and fry eggs lightly over a low heat. It's best to sprinkle them with a little water and steam them, covered, as the edges should not be crisp. Meanwhile, soften and heat tortillas on a lightly-greased griddle.

To serve, place 2 warmed and softened tortillas on each plate and top each with 1 fried egg. Cover with the hot *salsa*. Sprinkle with cheese and serve with *Refritos* (page 93). Serves 4.

The road from Oaxaca to Tehuantepec winds around and up and down, demanding the driver's full attention for hours so that a rest in Tehuantepec is almost a necessity. This is a stop much acclaimed in Mexico. It is near the turnoff to the highway than spans the narrowest distance between the west and east coasts, and the home of the beautiful and stately Tehuana women—if you can find them. The Tehuanas, who speak Zapotec, are pictured frequently in Mexican travel books and Spanish language textbooks. These women are reported to be the predominant force in the commerical and social life of the area. They are tall, with enviable posture, and dress picturesquely when they participate in the festivities of their region. They wear brightly colored embroidered skirts, boleros of velvet, much gold-coin jewelry, and a most extraordinary headdress that is tall and white with little dangling sleeves. There are several stories about the origin of this unusual headcover. The tale I like best relates that many years ago some Tehuana women found a trunk from a Spanish shipwreck at the nearby seaport of Salina Cruz. The trunk contained white infant baptismal gowns. The women thought they were head garments and adapted them to their festive dress, calling them *huipals*. They have been the customary head adornment ever since—or so the story goes.

In actuality, the town of Tehuantepec is not much to write home about. When we arrived it was a sand-blown day and it gave a yellowish cast to the town. (I understand that this is the climatic norm.) The best I can say, and it's enough, is that the *comida* in the local hotel was delicious *Puerco con Chile Verde* (Green Chile Pork), a dish that can be found in restaurants throughout the country. On this windy, weary afternoon it really hit the spot. I have adapted the recipe to canned *tomatillos* (green tomatoes) as they are widely available in Mexican markets and even in regular supermarkets in the United States and Canada.

PUERCO CON CHILE VERDE

(Green Chile Pork)

3 tablespoons shortening or oil
2 pounds lean pork, cubed into ½-inch pieces
1 medium onion, finely chopped
3 cloves garlic, mashed
2 *chiles jalapeños,* cored, seeded and minced

½ cup fresh cilantro, chopped
1 can (14-ounce) of Mexican green tomatoes (*tomatillos*) with liquid
1 teaspoon salt
Lime wedges

Heat oil in heavy skillet and add pork and onion. Cook over low-medium heat until pork is browned. Add all other ingredients (break up tomatoes) except lime, and simmer, covered, until pork is cooked through and tender (30 to 40 minutes). Taste and add more salt if desired. Serve with *Arroz Blanco* (page 37), warm corn tortillas (page 131), and lime wedges.

Driving out of the dry, breezy isthmus we kept on Highway 190 as it swung over to Tuxtla Gutiérrez, the capital of the state of Chiapas. A traveler coming this far south in Mexico will often push on to Guatemala, but Chiapas is an area well worth exploring first. Bordering on Oaxaca, the Pacific Ocean, and Guatemala, with the states of Veracruz and Tabasco to the east, it has a wide range of climate and topography. The tropical rain forest of Palenque is part of Chiapas, as is high, cool San Cristóbal de las Casas. Large parts of the jungles and forests of Chiapas are untouched, and there are surely wild animals and Mayan ruins yet unseen by contemporary eyes. The one well-known ruin, only accessible by train and muleback, is Bonampak. The trips and treks to visit this site originate in Tuxtla, and I think they would be well worth the time and expense for a stalwart fan of Mayan culture.

Tuxtla Gutiérrez is a business center for the coffee and tobacco production of the area. It's not a terribly pretty town, although there are a lot of flowers, fair accommodations, and a lively feeling. There are many interesting side trips from Tuxtla, though, that represent the diversity of the state. A few miles, to the north is the 6,000-foot deep El Sumidero Canyon, cut by the churning Río Chiapa that becomes the Río Grijalva as it flows into the Gulf of Mexico. I am quite content to view this treacherous gorge from a vista point, but it is possible to travel down the highway to Chiapa de Corzo and pick up a boat ride that goes a few miles into the canyon. I will always be sobered by the human history of El Sumidero. When the Spanish, in their attempt at southern conquest during the sixteenth century, reached the edge of the canyon, the Indians resisted, fighting until there was no more hope. Finally, in their proud refusal to be subjugated to Spanish rule, almost one thousand men, women, and children jumped to their deaths in El Sumidero. Needless to say, the Spanish took the message and made no more attempts to conquer Chiapas.

A few miles south of Tuxtla is the road that connects western and eastern Chiapas. Although recently paved, it still is not safe to drive during the rainy season. We took this road once to reach Palenque—one of the most breathtaking rides I have ever taken. Out of the chilly, winding, mountainous west and down into a tropical *barranca* that snakes through lush foilage with 100-foot waterfalls, we crossed back and forth over clear running streams and passed villages full of solemn faces and curious eyes. It must have been even more incredible for the *conquistadores* who, without a road and staggering in armor, pushed through all the way to Guatemala.

Back in Tuxtla and before we moved on south, we stopped for a little afternoon repast. Southern coastal Chiapas has many banana plantations and we tried *Platanos en Rompope,* a delicious dessert of sliced bananas soaked in *rompope*. This is a kind of alcoholic Mexican eggnog bottled and sold all over the country. It is very easy to make and, in my opinion, really tastes better than the commercial variety. With bananas it makes a delicious dessert served with *Cafe de Olla* (Pot Coffee), with or without *leche* (milk).

ROMPOPE
(Eggnog)

1 quart whole milk	10 egg yolks, beaten
1¼ cup sugar	1½ cups white rum
1 vanilla bean	

Combine milk, sugar, and vanilla bean in a saucepan and bring to a boil. Reduce heat and simmer, covered, for 20 minutes. Cool to room temperature, then remove the vanilla bean and beat egg yolks slowly into the milk mixture. Add rum, decant into bottles and cap or cork tightly. Refrigerate at least 48 hours before using. *Rompope* can be kept for months when refrigerated. Serve as a liqueur, warm or cold, or as a dessert when poured over fruit or ice cream. Makes about 1¾ quarts.

PLATANOS EN ROMPOPE
(Bananas in Rompope)

4 firm, but ripe medium-sized bananas	4 tablespoons finely-chopped almonds
2 cups *rompope,* warmed	

Slice thinly 1 banana into a dessert or compote dish and pour over ½ cup *rompope*. Into 3 other dishes, repeat procedure with remaining bananas and *rompope* and sprinkle each dish with 1 tablespoon ground almonds. Serves 4.

CAFÉ DE OLLA
(Pot Coffee)

1 quart water	1 3-inch stick cinnamon
½ cup dark-brown sugar, packed	⅓ cup dark roasted ground coffee

In a saucepan heat water, sugar, and cinnamon, and stir until sugar has melted. Add coffee. Bring mixture to a boil and reduce heat. Simmer for 4 to 5 minutes, then remove from heat. Strain through a fine strainer into a coffee server. Serve hot. Serves 4.

CAFÉ CON LECHE
(Coffee with Milk)

Make coffee as directed in *Café de Olla,* but use double the amount of ground coffee called for. Serve in large mugs combining ⅔ cup coffee with ⅔ cup hot milk.

The winding ascent on the fifty-mile drive from Tuxtla to San Cristóbal de las Casas is difficult when foggy, but beautiful when it's clear. Referred to as "Las Casas" by its residents, this very interesting village-city is named after Bartolomé de las Casas, a bishop who arrived in the mid-1600s and set to work to dispel Spanish myths about the Indians. He spent his life working in behalf of the native population, and quite successfully, which makes Las Casas an interesting place today.

Although Las Casas is full of Indians from the surrounding area, it is very Spanish in appearance with stone streets and old colonial buildings. Slender-faced Iberians and uniformed Catholic school children fall easily in step with the Zinacantecos and Chamulas in their distinguishing tunics, flat straw hats, and other variations in attire that identify them by tribe. I don't mean to romanticize Las Casas as the ideal in Spanish-Indian coexistence, but achieving the right balance seems to be an eternal dilemma for Mexico. (Taking the country as a whole, Mexicans are attempting to improve relations and the living conditions of the Indian population, and they certainly have come to recognize their Indian cultures as priceless natural resources.) It's nice to see that in a town as Spanish as Las Casas, in a state of Indian as Chiapas, the cultural contrasts are seemingly compatible.

For the most part, Las Casas is new to the tourist circuit, but there is a good market and many shops that carry Indian craft and clothing items. It's fun to browse around for that reason. We visited the market where the outlying Indians come to trade among themselves. We were looking for rope hammocks, which we didn't find, and caused quite a stir among the Indians, my brother and I both being tall even for *gringos*.

Two of my gastronomical memories of Las Casas were the *Tortilla Española* (Spanish Omelet) made with potatoes and chiles, and a light custard called *Jericalla* that has a pronounced cinnamon flavor. Both are easy to make, although I maintain Mexican potatoes cannot be equaled in taste or texture.

TORTILLA ESPAÑOLA
(Spanish Omelet)

4 tablespoons oil (olive oil is best)	2 *chiles jalapeños,* seeded, cored, and minced
½ cup finely-chopped onion	1 teaspoon salt
½ cup finely-chopped bell pepper	½ teaspoon oregano
2½ cups diced red potatoes with skins	8 eggs, beaten
	Lime wedges
	Sliced tomatoes

In a 10-inch frying pan or omelet pan, heat oil and sauté vegetables until all are softened. (Potatoes should be cooked through.) Stir in salt and oregano and pour in beaten eggs.

Cover mixture and cook over medium heat without stirring. When edge of the omelet begins to set, pull it in with a spatula and allow the uncooked eggs to flow to the outside. When the omelet is nearly set, place it under a broiler to firm and brown lightly. Cut into wedges and serve accompanied by lime wedges and tomato slices. Serves 4.

JERICALLA
(Cinnamon Custard)

½ cup sugar	2 cups milk
6 inches of cinnamon stick	3 eggs (4 if small)
	Powdered cinnamon

In a saucepan combine sugar and cinnamon with milk and bring to a boil. Remove from heat, cool slightly and cover. Refrigerate at least 8 hours. After chilling, preheat oven to 350°, reheat milk mixture in saucepan to a scald and remove cinnamon stick. In a bowl, beat eggs and then add milk mixture slowly, beating as you pour. Divide mixture among 4 custard cups and sprinkle tops lightly with powdered cinnamon. Set cups in a baking pan and add hot water to pan to reach to ½ the height of the dishes. Bake for about ½ hour or until custard is set. Chill or serve warm. Serves 4.

Central Chiapas presents an interesting trip for the Guatemala-bound. There are the villages of the surrounding Indians, and the lovely Lagos de Montebello (Montebello Lakes) to the east, a little drive and a short hike for the nature lover. However, this is a national sanctuary and not open to camping. The region is also the home of the Lacandon Indians, an isolated and ancient group of Mayas who have not ventured into the modern world until very recently, and then only lightly. They are distinguished from other Indians of the area by their long hair and white garments.

Some fifteen years ago I knew a young Canadian woman who had moved to the state of Guanajuato, but after visiting the jungles of Chiapas she went to live with the Lacandons and married the son of the chief. We lost track of her, but I learned recently from someone who had been doing a study of the Lacandons that she had left her husband, Chiapas, and Mexico— for reasons not clear. I guess it takes a long arm and a firm hand to cross all those borders.

CHAPTER SIX

❉

The Lakes and Valleys

PÁTZCUARO

*T*HE contrasts within Mexico are never so startling as during the drive between Toluca and Morelia, the capital city of Michoacán. A large part of this fertile state is covered with a rich, red earth that supports vast mountain forests, and large farms and ranches. In addition, the highway that links the two cities breaks through three national forests, and one of Mexico's largest lumber areas.

Coming off the high, arid plain around Toluca, a pine forest is the least of one's surprises. To further the contrast, a humid rain forest flourishes near San José Purúa, some seventy miles northwest of Toluca. I still find it hard to believe that within a few miles of windswept Highway 15 there is a tropical valley of mineral pools, waterfalls, and palm and banana trees, all splashed with lavender jacaranda, magenta bougainvillea, and delicate yellow hibiscus blossoms.

There are several mineral spas in the vicinity, the largest being the Hotel Spa San José Purúa which sits on the side of the deep, lush canyon. This hotel has over two hundred rooms, lovely landscaped grounds, and a large, warm (though murky) mineral pool. There are also two other pools for the public and the management offers free mineral jacuzzis and mud facials. This hotel is an old and reliable establishment and a fine find for the self-indulgent.

I stopped there with my niece some years ago and we took full advantage of the hotel's facilities. In the evening we sat in a small bar (one of several in the hotel) and sipped Margaritas while a warm but lively tropical storm lashed the window that looked out upon the valley below. So entranced was I by this hotel and the beauty around it, that I hoped to spend my birthday there several years later. At that time there was a tourist boycott of Mexico and the hotel was virtually empty. In

109

the gigantic dining room with its platoon of waiters hovering around, we felt like we belonged in some European caper movie.

On our first visit, Julie, my niece, wanted to try a dessert called *chongos,* but was hesitant to risk her evening *postre* on something she might not like. The waiter urged her to try it, offering to bring her another dessert with no charge if she didn't want it—he seemed to think she would love it. Well, the upshot was that she didn't like *chongos* very much and he kept his word—replacing it with a chocolate sundae. But I have grown to like this custard pudding, common to the state of Michoacán. Sometimes the recipe includes egg yolks but most often it is firmed with rennet alone.

CHONGOS
(Rennet Custard)

5 cups milk	2 tablespoons water
½ cup sugar	½ cup sugar
1 teaspoon vanilla	1 cinnamon stick
2 rennet tablets	

Mix milk with sugar and vanilla and heat to lukewarm. Remove from heat. Dissolve rennet tablets in water and add to milk mixture. Pour into round oven-proof dish or deep Pyrex dish and place in a warm spot until curd sets (about 40 minutes). When curd has set, cut into 1½-inch squares or into 6 pie wedges. Set pan on a very low heat (over a pad or star on the burner) and cook for 3 to 4 hours until the squares or shapes are firm like soft cheese. (The mixture should be kept on a low simmer, barely moving.) Remove curds gently with slotted spoon and put into an oven-proof dish or in individual, oven-proof dessert dishes. Transfer 1½ cups of whey to a saucepan and add sugar and cinnamon. Bring to a boil and continue to boil for 2 to 3 minutes. Remove cinnamon stick and pour sugar mixture gently over *chongos.* Cool to lukewarm and serve or serve chilled. Serves 6.

Morelia is a charming city, relatively quiet and relatively large (over 200,000). Established in the mid-sixteenth century, it was known as Vallodolid until 1828 when the name was changed to Morelia to honor José María Morelos, the Catholic priest who was defrocked and executed after participating in the Mexican revolution against Spain.

Morelia is a lovely city for the traveler. It's colonial in feeling with beautiful homes and regal public buildings of pink stone, trimmed in traditional ironwork. (This is another city with an ordinance that requires all new construction to be consistent with old-world architecture.) Coming into the city from Toluca you pass a mile-long aqueduct that was built in the late eighteenth century. It's a most unusual piece of engineered masonry, thirty feet high with 250-some arches.

Like the cities in the bajío, Morelia is conservative and Catholic with a number of interesting historical stops. One that is worth a glance is the College of San Nicolas Obispo, the second oldest educational institution in Mexico. (The first is the National University in Mexico City.) The school was founded in 1540, although its first location was in Pátzcuaro. Morelia was the intellectual base for not only Father Morelos, but also Miguel Hidalgo, the controversial priest who was most responsible for organizing the beginnings of the 1810 revolution against Spain. It was at San Nicolás that Father Hidalgo earned his nickname "the fox" because of his great gift for rhetoric.

Another interesting stop is the Casa de Morelos, a museum now but actually the home where Father Morelos was born. Among personal items on display is the blindfold that covered his eyes when he was shot. A short distance from the museum is the Plaza Principal, the lovely tree-shaded city center, which is surrounded by restaurants under the portals. Here tourists and residents stop to sip and chat. And what better place to enjoy a warming cup of Mexican chocolate on a brisk morning!

Chocolate is as Mexican as corn. Long before the Spanish arrived, cacao beans were cultivated for making a drink brewed with water. In fact, chocolate comes from a Nahuatal word which means "bitter water." One of the more common craft items found in Mexico is the *molinillo,* the carved wooden

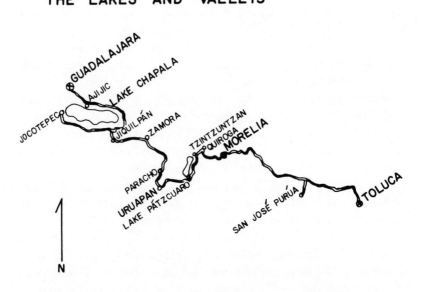

beater that whips the chocolate drink into a froth. Chocolate, for both eating and drinking, comes in bars or rounds pressed with cinnamon and sugar, vanilla and sugar, or almonds and sugar. In my opinion, its flavor outranks any we have in the United States because I favor dark, heavy chocolate. We do import some Mexican drinking chocolate, but if you do not have a local source here is a recipe that makes a fair imitation.

CHOCOLATE CALIENTE
(Hot Chocolate)

1½ ounce unsweetened chocolate	½ teaspoon vanilla
2 cups milk	5 heaping teaspoons brown sugar
⅛ teaspoon ground cinnamon	

Melt chocolate over a low heat or over water in a double boiler. Stir in milk, cinnamon, vanilla, and sugar. Heat through and beat to a froth with a *molinillo,* egg beater, or in a blender. Serve immediately in mugs. Makes 2 cups.

As I mentioned before, I have had some very excellent pork in Morelia. (It seems that pork is tasty all over Mexico.) Another dish I associate with Morelia is *Adobo Rojo de Lomo de Cerdo* (pork loin in a red chile sauce). This recipe is delicious and easy to prepare.

ADOBO ROJO DE LOMO DE CERDO
(Pork Loin in *Adobo* Sauce)

3 pounds lean boneless pork loin, cut into 2-inch pieces	1 cinnamon stick
	2 whole cloves
	2 peppercorns
1 small onion	¼ teaspoon cumin seed
Water	½ teaspoon oregano
6 *chiles anchos*	2 garlic cloves
1 cup water	1 teaspoon salt
½ cup vinegar	

In a pot, put pork and whole onion and cover with water. Bring to a boil, cover, and simmer for 1½ hours until pork is tender. Pour off broth and retain. Meanwhile, toast chiles lightly over a flame, then core, seed and devein. Put chiles in a saucepan with water, vinegar, and cinnamon stick. Simmer, covered, for 25 minutes, then transfer to blender. Grind cloves, peppercorns, and cumin seed in a spice grinder or crush in a mortar. Add to the blender along with oregano, garlic, and salt. Transfer cooked onion from pork pot to blender and blend together all ingredients. Pour blended sauce over pork and heat through. Add a little of the pork broth if necessary but sauce should be thick enough to stick to the meat. Serve with *Arroz Blanco* (page 37). Serves 4.

The most interesting route to Lake Pátzcuaro is through the town of Quiroga, and the village of Tzintzuntzan (say it without the t's). There is a stretch of road that is lined with trees, poplar, I think, which always brings back to me a story I heard years ago from an American woman living in Mexico. She said that during the government's persecution of the church in the 1920s there was a time when a priest or nun was hanged from every tree along the road. It's a terrifying story and hard to forget. But, I don't think it is quite true even though the reaction to the church at that time was much more oppressive than one can imagine—Mexico being so Catholic.

Quiroga is named after Bishop Vasco de Quiroga who worked so hard for the Indians in his area by developing the crafts of each village. (He also established the first College of Saint Nicolás.) Even today this area is a wonderland for the shopper, especially those interested in folk art and craft. While Quiroga is a real town, pleasant and busy with many shops and a good market, Tzintzuntzan is more of a stop in the road. At one time, Tzintzuntzan was the capital of the Tarascan Indians, a proud people who were some of the last to resist the Spanish domination. The name of the village is Tarascan for "place of the hummingbird"—a musical-sounding name and an appropriate one here. This is where the Tarascan kings were buried, presumably in robes made of hummingbird wings. Pyramids are visible from the road, although the village functions mainly as a tourist stop where regional pottery and other crafts are sold in little stalls on the road. This is one of my favorite pauses in Mexico, commercial as it is. The people, descendents of the early Tarascans, are very friendly.

Pátzcuaro, too, is full of Tarascan heritage. This is truly one of the "musts" of Mexico and I know I will never tire of visiting the area. Perhaps I should interject a comment about the "sameness" of Mexican towns and villages. I think the reason for the traveler's response—"if you have seen one Mexican town you have seen them all"—is simply because there is a family resemblance. As I mentioned before, most communities are laid out in a grid, interrupted always by one central plaza and sometimes several other little squares, depending on the size of the town. These plazas are plain or fancy, relative to the wealth in the local treasury. They may have benches, trees, flowers, and/or grass. Frequently there is a bandstand in the center. Couples, males and females, sometimes two of the same sex, link arms and stroll around the plaza in the evening, chatting and laughing. It's definitely the center and the pulse of the community. On one side of the plaza there is a church, occasionally modest, but often ornate beyond the seeming means of the town. The other sides are filled with shops, restaurants, and walkways under portals where more activity takes place. The buildings in some towns are painted in high color, others—especially in the northern and western ranch areas—maintain a dull adobe.

At this point the similarities end and the regional culture and geography take over. Pátzcuaro has all of the above and its own wonderful style, too. The town is built on a slope overlooking a deep blue-green lake that is surrounded by hills, some forested, some cleared. The lake is not for swimming as it is sedgy around the shore, but is filled with boats and fishermen catching the prolific white fish, the star of the local cuisine. These fish are caught with beautiful butterfly-shaped nets that are said to have been designed by Bishop Quiroga. (When my son was small, we bought him a little carved toy version of the boats and net. It was an exquisite piece of work and a great favorite in the bathtub.)

In the middle of Lake Pátzcuaro is a little island named Janitzio, a colorful fishing village built around a large white sculpture of the revered José Morelos (you can walk up inside of it). Visitors to Pátzcuaro can take one of the frequent launches over to the island—it only takes a half hour or so, and the villagers welcome tourists. Again, it is one of those guide-book standards, but a lovely excursion.

The streets of Pátzcuaro are cobbled and many of the buildings are old and of colonial style. The town market is a good browse with lots of wood and copper items for sale. I bought a pair of carved salad servers many years ago that I still use regularly—and I remember that they were less than ten cents each. Although it is basically a tourist market, the people from the hills around come also to sell and trade among themselves. There is so much available because of the many little craft villages nearby. One popular item is the handwoven cotton cloth called *cambaya* which is available by the yard from bolts or made up into clothing, tablecloths, napkins and bedspreads. The plain colors, stripes, plaids, and checks are all beautiful. This fabric is one of the major reasons for my visiting Pátzcuaro time and time again.

Pescado blanco, the white fish of Lake Pátzcuaro, is a specialty of the restaurants in and around the town. The method of preparation can be duplicated for any white fish fillets. Also peculiar to the area around both the Lakes Pátzcuaro and Chapala in Jalisco is *sangrita.* This is a spicy little concoction that is drunk alternately with a sip of tequila, both served in small glasses. We were so pleased the first time we tried *sangrita* with the white fish that we asked for the recipe and also hunted down the glasses in which it should be served. It was a very chilly night in Pátzcuaro and we walked all over the town until we found the store that sold these special little glasses.

PESCADO BLANCO ESTILO DE PÁTZCUARO
(White fish Pátzcuaro-style)

2 medium-size onions, thinly sliced	Salt and pepper
¼ cup oil	Oil
¾ cup white wine vinegar	4 large white fish fillets
⅓ cup lime juice	Shredded lettuce
3 eggs	Sliced tomatoes
¼ cup flour	Lime wedges.

Spread onions in a pan and pour oil and vinegar over them. Simmer until onions are clear, then cool and chill for garnish. Beat together lime juice, eggs, and flour, salt and pepper. Heat about ¼ inch oil in a heavy frying pan, dip fillets in egg mixture and fry on both sides until crisp and golden-brown. Garnish with pickled onions, shredded lettuce, and tomatoes. Serve with lime wedges. Serves 4.

SANGRITA

2 cups orange juice	Salt
¼ cup lime juice	Crushed tiny red chiles
¼ cup grenadine	(*chile pequín*) to taste

Mix together all ingredients and chill. Serve in small glasses with corresponding glasses of tequila. Serves 4.

A swing into real Tarascan country from Pátzcuaro will take the traveler through the city of Uruapan, know for its remarkable lacquer work and its proximity to the silent volcano, Paricutín. What makes Paricutín interesting is that it only appeared in 1943 when a farmer noticed smoke rising from the ground and felt heat under his feet. He rushed away to get a priest but by the time they returned to the field, a giant hole had erupted. Rather quickly the volcano swallowed up the nearby villages and in the subsequent ten years it grew some 4,000 feet and frequently terrorized the people in the area.

Uruapan means "flower place" in the Tarascan language, and the town and surrounding area are lush with flowers, tropical foliage, banana and orange groves. I remember a lot of birds in Uruapan, but maybe it's because they are so often painted on the lacquer objects made there. I also found it interesting that iguana meat is sold widely in this area. On a later trip to Uruapan we drove up from Playa Azul on the coast and stopped to look over Presa El Infiernillo (The Chafing Dish Dam). There were iguanas all over the hill on which we were standing. They are startling, but I understand the meat is as tender and mild as young fowl. I've yet to try it.

As a child in southern California, Mexican lacquered trays and *jícaras,* the bowls made from gourds, were the most common of tourist items found in the border towns. They seemed so commercial to me, and it wasn't until I visited Uruapan and realized the intricacies of the craft that I developed a proper respect for the lacquered goods. The old method—I don't know if it is still used—was to rub the wood with a lacquer made up of oil of wild sage, oil from a small local insect, and dolomite, a magnesia-rich soft rock. The applications are done in stages and layers and make a very strong, waterproof finish. At some point the designs are etched in (mostly flowers and birds of the area) and then painted before more lacquer is applied. Other places in Mexico produce lacquered goods, but Uruapan remains the best known.

Heading now toward Lake Chapala and Guadalajara we pass through Paracho, a town interesting alone for its wooden buildings. However, Paracho is better known to North American music lovers as the center of guitar making. Various kinds of wooden string instruments are made in Paracho, but the guitars are most famous and the craft is carried on through generations of families. It's apparently full of musical people as it is known for its folk music, too.

Halfway between Uruapan and the lake is Zamora (home of *chongos*) where the motorist can make the decision to drive along the southern or northern side of the lake. I like to cut to the southern side to stop in Jiquilpan with its thoroughly non-tourist atmosphere. (I have never been so stared at as in the market in Jiquilpan.) It is the birthplace of one of this century's most honorable presidents, Lazaro Cárdenas, and his house on the main street is marked—although it isn't open to the public. It's a nicely dignified town with lots of trees and a river running through the center. There is an old library with a dark wood interior, an Orozco mural on the wall, and tables with shaded reading lamps attached. With the somberness of its antiquity and the stress of the mural, it has the atmosphere of a church.

Jiquilpan has a hotel where I love to stay. It has had the same gentlemanly proprietor for the fifteen years I have been going there, but the hotel rarely has many guests. Although the rooms are old, they are spacious with bedsteads and vanities painted in brightly colored stripes. The bathrooms are gigantic and immaculate but the towels are thin and the plumbing a bit unpredictable. Still, it is a wonderfully restful place and the dining room serves delicious food. I think they cater mostly to local people because the guests always seem friendly with each other. On our last visit we had pork *flautas*. A *flauta* means flute and the idea is to roll corn tortillas tightly around a filling of pork (or chicken or sausage or beef) and then fry them. They are then garnished with *guacamole* and *crema* and eaten with the fingers. That day, *flautas* were served with *Arroz Verde* (Green Rice) and sliced tomatoes.

FLAUTAS DE PUERCO
(Pork Flutes)

12 corn tortillas	Oil or lard for frying
2 cups shredded pork	*Guacamole* (page 157)
(page 79)	*Crema* (see below)

Use two tortillas for each *flauta*. To roll, soften them by heating in a hot, ungreased griddle or over a low flame or coil. Lay flat 2 overlapping tortillas and spoon a narrow strip of meat down the middle of the tortillas. Roll tightly and secure with a toothpick. Fry them each in ½ inch of hot oil or lard. Serve hot, garnished with *Guacamole* and *Crema,* and with *Arroz Verde* (page 120). Makes 6 *flautas*.

CREMA
(Mexican Soured Cream)

2 cups heavy cream	3 tablespoons buttermilk
(whipping cream)	or sour cream

Mix together cream and buttermilk or sour cream in a crockery or glass container. Let mixture sit in a warm place for 8 to 12 hours or until thickened. (It will thicken more with chilling.)

Refrigerate and serve as whipped cream on desserts or as sour cream on entrées. Makes 2 cups.

ARROZ VERDE
(Green Rice)

2 cups long-grain white rice	1 *chile serrano,* stemmed and chopped
1 cup chopped parsley	1 clove garlic
3 sprigs cilantro	⅓ cup oil
½ cup chopped, green onions	1 teaspoon salt
2 large dark-green lettuce leaves	4 cups chicken broth

Put rice in a bowl and cover with hot water. Leave 15 minutes, then drain and rinse with cold water until the water runs clear of starch. Drain well and set aside. In blender, purée parsley, cilantro, onions, lettuce, chile, and garlic. Heat oil in heavy-bottomed pan, add rice, and stir to coat rice grains. Add purée and continue to stir and fry until rice is quite dry. Mix salt with broth and pour over rice. Stir once and then lower heat to simmer. Cover and steam for 20 minutes without stirring until water is absorbed and rice is tender. Serves 5 to 6.

Lake Chapala is very large although for some years it was receding at an alarming rate. Apparently the state water engineers rallied because the lake is now fuller than it's been in awhile. Fed originally by the Lerma River, this tranquil lake is a nice experience for the traveler as you can drive nearly its circumference with an undisturbed view of the water. The southern side is less populated than the Guadalajara side which has three pretty lakeside towns, Chapala, Ajijic, and Jocotepec. The first two are especially popular with tourists, and with immigrants from the United States and Canada. Jocotepec is a little more "native." One evening some years ago we attended a traveling fair in Jocotepec. It was fun wandering around the various concessions watching the expressions of pure joy on the faces of the children. We marveled at the abandon of the Mexican soul as the townspeople climbed into the popular double ferris wheel, balanced precariously on rocks that I could move even by myself. It's not ususual for these jerrybuilt structures to collapse, and not for all the *pesos* in Pátzcuaro would I have risked a ride on that one.

On the less hazardous level I should insert the recipe here for *Sopa de Albóndigas,* a meatball soup that I had in Chapala. This is the queen of soups in Mexico, and the state of Jalisco claims it as its own.

SOPA DE ALBÓNDIGAS
(Meatball Soup)

1 pound lean ground beef	1 teaspoon salt
1 small onion, minced	½ teaspoon thyme
1 cup soft bread crumbs	¼ teaspoon nutmeg
⅓ cup pine nuts (optional)	2 quarts rich beef broth
1 egg, lightly beaten	1 bay leaf
⅓ cup milk	⅓ cup medium-dry sherry
	Chiles serranos, chopped
	Lime wedges

Mix together beef, onion, bread crumbs and pine nuts with a fork. Mix egg, milk, and seasonings and stir into meat mixture until all is well mixed. Heat broth with bay leaf and shape meat mixture into small balls. Gently drop meatballs into simmering broth and cook, covered, for 25 to 30 minutes. Just before serving stir in sherry. Serve soup with a small bowl of chopped chiles and lime wedges. Serves 6.

Guadalajara is one of Mexico's largest and finest cities. It was once second in population, although recently it has been edged into third by Monterrey. Founded in 1535 as the capital of the province of Nueva Galicia, Guadalajara has all the trappings of its colonial beginning. For the first-time visitor to Mexico it is a good choice as it combines the most prominent features of the country—the exciting mariachi music (with the song "Guadalajara" being a real spine tingler), colonial architecture, and the wonderful mixture of Spanish tradition and Indian mysticism. It also has marvelous restaurants.

Guadalajara is efficient also in the modern sense, catering to a new middle class and a large colony of foreign residents, especially Americans. It's not difficult to figure out the downtown configuration, but the city as a whole can be confusing as many streets turn and change names. I don't know how many times I have been through Guadalajara, and though I can find the bus or train station, a favorite hotel, or restaurant, I always get lost looking for places in the outer rings. But it's a nice city to lose yourself in if you aren't intimidated by frequent displays of *machismo* behind the wheel.

Guadalajara has its share of impressive churches, but the most remarkable is the cathedral located near the center of the city. It's a strange combination of styles due to stops and starts in construction and an earthquake that damaged it, but it houses some impressive art, including the famous painting "The Assumption of the Virgin" by Esteban Murillo. East of the cathedral is the Degollado Theater which is ornate Spanish in style, with crystal chandeliers and red and gold wall coverings. It is the home of the Guadalajara Symphony, although many other performances are given there.

Also in Guadalajara is the Orozco Museum (*El Museo Orozco*), which actually was the workshop of José Clemente Orozco, one of Mexico's most famous muralists. Within are almost a hundred of his paintings (there are Orozco murals in other buildings in the city also.) I like museums and I think their state museum (Guadalajara is the capital of Jalisco) is a good one. It contains both Spanish and Mexican paintings, many regional crafts, and some generally interesting historical things, including the carriage that belonged to the Emperor Maximilian. There is more to be seen for the craft-oriented in the *Casa de las Artesanías de Jalisco* (the state artisans house). This is a good study in regional crafts including the blown glass of this area.

The process of glassblowing can be watched in nearby Tlaquepaque (saying "clockie pockie" produces a horrible accent, but is more or less the pronunciation.) Although the central market in Guadalajara is full of buys for the tourists (it extends for blocks), Tlaquepaque is an Olympic event. This little village is nothing but shops and eateries.

Guadalajara is indeed a gourmand's delight. Every dish prepared in the republic is duplicated here along with their own specialties. Two things I favored were *Pozole,* the popular pork and hominy stew, and *Chayotes Rellenos,* stuffed *chayotes,* a pear-shaped vegetable that is prepared in many different ways in Mexico. Although *Pozole* is traditionally made with a pig's head, I fix it with pork loin ribs and get a good broth just the same. I don't think *Pozole* was made with oregano in Guadalajara, but I like it better with a little added.

POZOLE
(Pork and Hominy Stew)

2 *chiles anchos*
2 pounds lean and meaty
  pork ribs (loin is
  preferable)
1 teaspoon salt
6 chicken thighs or legs
3 cloves garlic, mashed

1 teaspoon oregano
3 tablespoons red wine
  vinegar
2 cans (1-pound each)
  white hominy drained
Salt and pepper to taste

GARNISHES:

Shredded lettuce or
  cabbage
Chopped cilantro

Sliced radishes
Chopped scallions
Lime wedges

Seed and devein chiles, break into pieces and cover with water to soften. Put ribs in a large heavy pot and cover amply with water. Bring to a boil, reduce heat, salt and simmer for 1½ to

2 hours. Add chicken. (If water is cooking down add a little more boiling water to the pot.) Continue to simmer for another ½ hour or until chicken is tender. Drain off broth, cool, and refrigerate until fat hardens on the top and is easy to remove. Put a small amount of broth in blender with chiles, garlic, oregano, and vinegar. Blend until smooth and add with remaining broth and hominy to chicken and pork. Simmer together for another 40 minutes. Salt and pepper to taste and serve stew in large bowls. Garnishes should be served in separate bowls to add to stew at the table. Serves 6.

CHAYOTES RELLENOS
(Stuffed *Chayotes*)

2 *chayotes*	¼ teaspoon salt
2 tablespoons minced onion	Pepper
	Cayenne pepper
1 egg, beaten	
½ cup white cheese, (Farmers, Monterey Jack), grated	

Cover whole *chayotes* with hot water and bring to a boil. Reduce heat and simmer until fork tender, but not too soft (about 20 minutes). Cut in half lengthwise and save half with seeds to use as garnish. Cut a line about ¼ inch in from the outside of the other *chayote* half and scoop out flesh, leaving a shell to stuff. Put scooped-out flesh in blender and purée. Transfer to a small bowl and mix with onions, egg, cheese, salt, and pepper. Heap into *chayote* shells and sprinkle with cayenne pepper. Bake in a 350° oven for about 20 minutes to set. Set half with seeds on top of the filled half before serving. Serves 4 as a first course or use as a side dish.

CHAPTER SEVEN

The Bajío

GUANAJUATO

THE ride from Guadalajara into the historic and fertile *bajío* (lowlands) is easy and pleasant. The main routes pass through quiet, small towns and rolling ranchlands with only a slightly noticeable gain in altitude. Actually, this is not low country at all. It is just a little lower than Mexico City, and is the drainage basin for the Lerma River, one of the best farming regions of the country.

This is the part of Mexico I know and love best, having spent many months at different intervals in the area near Guanajuato, the capital city of the state of the same name. The large, broad paddle cactus called *nopal* grows throughout Mexico and is common in illustrations about Mexico or painted on souvenirs but I always think of this central area as being the land of *nopal* because it is so abundant. In southern Guanajuato, especially, these plants are grown as hedge fences around small ranchos, and as property divisions in the villages. This cactus and the lacy, drooping *pirul* trees are my favorite botanical links with this tranquil area, along with the occasional flashes of color from the sturdy geranium bushes and the bougainvillea vines.

The strawberry fields around the city of Irapuato in the state of Guanajuato are a good example of the fertility of the *bajío*. Said to be the largest strawberry-producing area in the world, the fruit is shipped all over from here. Along the roads, little family stands sell fresh berries in tall baskets, and jars of *mermelada de fresas* (strawberry jam).

The colonial city of Guanajuato is one of the most exquisite in the country. Not a grid at all, the city lies in a deep crease in the mountains and is built up and down the sides of this ravine. Except for the residences of the very wealthy, the houses are small and cube shaped, sharing common walls and built directly on the edges of the cobbled streets.

The façades of Mexican homes are commonly plain, although in certain areas where there is more money and Spanish influence, the fronts are often decorated with wrought iron, and the doors are large and heavily carved. Most of the homes are built around central patios in the Mediterranean style, and a glimpse into even the most modest *casa* will reveal a lovely patio with flowers and trees growing profusely, and dogs and children playing around the sunlit center. (Incidentally, it's not difficult to take a peek as the doors are often open. Mexicans like to stand in doorways to greet friends and watch the street action.)

Many of the houses in Guanajuato are painted in bright colors and warm pastels, and flowerpots hang from the eaves or sit on the window sills. All the streets were once cobbled, or laid with paving stones, but now some have been paved with asphalt. However, they have not been widened since the horse-drawn era and as a result, Guanajuato is almost totally routed one-way. When we first arrived, we had a small station wagon that barely slipped between the buildings on either side of the street by the university. This was the route to the post office and, in time, I became very adept at driving rather rapidly (no cross streets) down this very narrow road. University students standing or walking on the thin strand of sidewalk on either side of the street were accustomed to flattening themselves against the buildings to avoid being bumped by passing vehicles.

Once a river ran through the city, but some years ago an ambitious governor decided to reroute it into underground pipes and turn the river bed into a subterranean road. Visitors to the city are always fascinated at driving under the city between stone walls. Unfortunately, there is an engineering problem in this design. A sudden, heavy rain, bringing a big runoff into the city will often flood this underground road and tear up the pavement.

The central market of Guanajuato was my first introduction to the mysterious ingredients used in Mexican cuisine, and it is still my favorite market. It is housed in a gigantic building with a curved ceiling of paned glass. The tables in the middle of the first floor are covered with fresh produce, eggs, and dairy products, and the sides of the building are lined with dry goods stalls and meat markets. Upstairs, a balcony is packed with souvenir items because Guanajuato is popular with Mexican as well as foreign tourists. Looking down from the balcony, the food floor is a great wash of colors, and there is (typical of all Mexican markets) the pervading earthy smell of fresh cilantro, mingled with the sweet odors of ripe fruit, dried *chiles,* and fresh meat. Very little food is kept sealed or packaged and as a result the smells in Mexico are wonderful and I am never offended by odors there—except perhaps by the industrial smells on the outskirts of some of the large cities.

On the outside of the market are open-air restaurants which add to the wonderful odors of the interior. These restaurant kitchens, makeshift by our standards, turn out some wonderful dishes and operate from early morning until late in the night. This brings up an interesting point about Mexican cooking. The beautiful, tiled kitchen is not common except in the homes of the very wealthy and in many families the cooking is still done on a wood stove or over a charcoal brazier. Also, not many of the poorer people have refrigeration. Kitchen appliances, though increasing in use, still are quite antiquated to our eyes, and large ranges are rare even in middle-class homes. The most

THE BAJÍO

common new appliances are apartment-sized stoves and double hot plates.

When we were first living in a village outside Guanajuato, a woman who worked for us lived down the street with her daughter, grandchildren, and aged mother. They cooked (on a charcoal stove), ate, and slept in one small room, and despite the conditions, she could turn out the most wonderful dishes. On the first night of one of our return visits, her grandson, a playmate of my son, brought us a plate of delicious *Enchiladas de Queso Blanco en Salsa Roja* (White Cheese Enchiladas in Red Sauce) so nicely presented with lettuce and radish garnish. It still amazes me when I think of what she had to work with compared to every kitchen I have known.

ENCHILADAS DE QUESO BLANCO EN SALSA ROJA
(White Cheese Enchiladas in Red Sauce)

6 *chiles anchos*	2 eggs, beaten
1½ cups hot water	12 corn tortillas
4 medium tomatoes, peeled, cored, and seeded	½ cup lard or oil
	½ pound crumbled *queso fresco* (page 96)*
1 large onion, chopped	1 cup sour cream or
2 cloves garlic	*crema* (page 119)
3 tablespoons lard or oil	Shredded lettuce
	Sliced radishes
Salt	

Core, seed, and devein chiles. Break into pieces and cover with hot water for 2 hours. Put in a blender with tomatoes, onion, and garlic and blend until smooth. In a frying pan, fry chile purée in lard or oil for 3 to 5 minutes. Salt to taste, add eggs, stir, and remove red sauce from heat but keep warm. Soften each tortilla in 2 teaspoons lard or oil and dip into red sauce. Fill tortilla with crumbled cheese, roll, and place in a baking

*A soft, dry, white cheese like Farmers, Muenster, or Monterey Jack can be substituted.

dish. These rolls should be placed close together and kept warm while filling all tortillas. Reheat remaining sauce and pour over enchiladas. Cover dish tightly with foil or a lid and place in a 350° oven for 12 to 15 minutes to heat through. Serve immediately dribbled with a little sour cream or *crema* and garnished with shredded lettuce and sliced radishes. Makes 12 enchiladas.

This same family was very kind to my son and were greatly responsible for developing in him a love of Mexican cooking. When he was not yet five, he would watch the grandmother and her daughter pat out tortillas and cook them on the traditional *comal*. They were very patient and often he would come home with some lumpy, grimy, little tortillas they had let him make. I laughed until I tried to make them myself. Hand patting is a marvel to me still, and I never attempt making tortillas without a tortilla press.

Tortilla shops, making hand-shaped tortillas, have long been replaced by machinery. Even small towns and villages have tortilla factories now, and in recent years in Guanajuato a little truck circles through the outlying areas almost every day bringing fresh, hot tortillas to those who have not been able to get into town. The freshly made tortilla is another one of the wonderful smells of Mexico.

There is considerable variation in tortillas. Not only are there the different tasting wheat-flour tortillas of the northwest, but some of the tortillas in more remote areas also look different because they are made from multi-colored corn. The following recipe is for corn tortillas made from the corn flour called *masa harina* which is sold in American markets. While it takes a little time to perfect tortilla making, be reassured that handling does not make them heavy. After all, they are a hand operation from the beginning. And control your impulse to salt the dough. The traditional taste is unsalted as tortillas are used primarily as scoops for salted foods.

TORTILLAS DE MAIZ

(Corn Tortillas)

2 cups *masa harina* (corn flour)	1¼ cups water

Mix the *masa* and water to make a soft dough, then heat a griddle or *comal* over a medium-high flame. Divide dough into 12 sections and roll into even balls. Flatten balls slightly. Put each piece between two pieces of wax paper or plastic in a tortilla press and flatten carefully to about 3½ inches in diameter. (Watch the edges and if they begin to split apart, you should add a bit more water. If it is too difficult to pull the dough away from the paper or plastic the dough may have too much water.) Place the tortillas on the hot griddle or *comal* until the edges begin to dry slightly. (Don't leave it on too long or the edge curls up.) Flip it over once and let it cook until it gets unevenly brown. The top of the tortilla may begin to puff up but don't encourage this unless you are using the tortilla for stuffing (see *Panuchos con Pavo* page 59). Flatten it lightly with the spatula and turn it over once more to brown slightly on the first side. Keep the tortilla warm and completely covered while you are making the others. Serve warm. Makes 12 tortillas.

One of my early memories of the Guanajuato market is of the *gelatina* and *flan* venders who carried trays, sometimes on their heads, of little plastic molds of vibrant-colored gelatin and the light, classic Spanish custard called *flan.* My son was delighted by the colors of the *gelatinas,* but like his favorite *paletas* (like Popsicles), they were often made with tap water and the indulgence was risky business.

Flan is a big favorite in Mexico and it is made with several flavorings. The simple *flan* with the caramel coating is still *numero uno* and I doubt there is a restaurant in the republic that does not have *flan* as a standard feature on its menu.

FLAN SENCILLO
(Simple Flan)

1½ cups sugar	⅛ teaspoon salt
1 quart milk	4 whole eggs
2 teaspoons vanilla	6 egg yolks

Preheat oven to 350°. In a heavy-bottomed saucepan, heat ¾ cup of the sugar over a moderately high heat. Stir until sugar has melted and turns a golden caramel color (8 to 10 minutes.) Pour into a mold and quickly coat the sides and bottom of the mold. (Syrup will harden rapidly so you must be fast.) Set aside to cool; it will harden like toffee but soften in baking.

Put milk in another saucepan with remaining sugar, vanilla, and salt and simmer for about 15 minutes. (Milk will reduce some.) Cool milk mixture, beat eggs with egg yolks, add to cooled milk and pour all into coated mold. Place mold in a pan containing water deep enough to come ½ way up the sides of the mold and bake in preheated oven. Remove from oven when a knife, inserted in the center of the *flan,* comes out clean. (In a flat pan this will take a little over 1 hour, in a tall, standard *flan* mold it will take closer to 2 hours.) Cool baked *flan* and then refrigerate. Bring to room temperature before unmolding and serving. (If *flan* does not slither around in the pan and unmold easily put mold in a little warm water to release caramel from the mold.) Serve inverted with caramel on top. Serves 8.

At the front entrance of the market building in Guanajuato is a most unusual rack of candy—doll-sized mummies made of taffy, dressed as men, women, and children, and wrapped in bright cellophane. These are popular tourist items and one of the most extraordinary combinations of culture and cuisine that you will see in Mexico.

They do have their story though, one that never fails to send shivers down the travelers' spine. The municipal cemetery is called *el panteón,* and the one in Guanajuato, like most Mexican graveyards, is crowded with elaborate headstones and monuments. For centuries, it was the custom for families to rent grave space for the deceased, and by law, the body could stay entombed for the first five years even if the family had not paid the rent. Then, if after these five years there had been no payment, the body was unearthed and put into a common grave. This custom is no longer followed, but it continued into this century.

In Guanajuato, because of the dryness of the air and the chemical composition of the soil, bodies do not completely decompose—enough, however, that after some years they are surely mummies and quite grotesque. In time, someone saw the commercial value of some of these relics, which were stacked up against a wall in an underground crypt, and began to advertise them as a tourist attraction. (This is Mexico, after all.) Now, *las momias de Guanajuato* are displayed in glass cases in a highly-lit building above ground, and are as big a draw as the beautiful churches, the market, and the elegant neo-classic *Teatro Juárez* combined. Every day people file through the building and stare with more interest than horror at these cases of contorted figures, their adobe-colored skin stiffened over fleshless bones. Some of the mummies have tufts of dry hair on their heads or behind their ears, and are wearing clothes so aged and tattered that they are falling off the shrunken frames. A few of the children have dolls or toys in their hands. Outside there is a parking lot rimmed with food concessions and booths selling mummy souvenirs, including the same kind of candy found at the market. This is truly one of the wonders of Mexico.

Perhaps a little general history about Guanajuato is in order here since the city is so antique and figured heavily in both the colonial and revolutionary periods of the country. Guanajuato is a bastardized bit of Spanish for the Tarascan name, Quanax-auto, which means "hill of frogs," so named because of two rocks in the area that resemble frogs. The present city grew out of several settlements that were part of an area granted to Don Rodrigo Vásquez in 1546 in payment for his dutiful services to the Spanish crown. The towns merged after 1550 when silver was discovered by a muleteer who found the precious metal under his campsite. This original discovery led to the eventual find of three true silver veins in the area and made Guanajuato, until the end of the nineteenth century, one of the major silver-producing regions of the world.

During the nineteenth century a number of influences slowed down the mines—labor costs, technical problems, the constant threat of floods in the mine shafts, and the oppressive physical conditions that led to the early demise of some of the miners.

The process of extracting additional ore from the mined earth was no more healthy for the miner than working underground. Referred to as the "patio process," the already mined earth was spread out in a large circle—about fifty feet in diameter and piled to a depth of about two feet. Mercury was then dropped by hand by Indian workers over and over, and after a time the silver and mercury amalgamated. The shininess of the mercury made the silver easy to see and pick up but needless to say, mercury poisoning among the workers was common.

Another factor in the eventual decline of the silver boom in Guanajuato was the battle at the *Alhóndiga* in 1810. The *Alhóndiga de Granaditas* was the gigantic grain storehouse built on a hill above the present market site. In September 1810, Padre Miguel Hidalgo y Costilla, the outspoken parish priest of nearby Dolores, in an attempt to put an end to colonial oppression, declared war on Spanish rule in Mexico. With the assistance of two Spanish officers, Captains Ignazio José Allende and Juan Aldama, of the San Miguel garrison, they rounded up soldiers and hundreds of discontented Indians for a march across the *bajío*. In the ensuing drama, this crowd with little discipline and in much disorder sacked the towns of San Miguel, Salamanca, Celaya, Irapuato, and Silao, swelling the ranks of revolutionaries along the way to somewhere over 20,000. They finally reached Guanajuato, the richest city in the area, and asked for a surrender of the city. When the mayor refused (assuming military help was on the way), Padre Hidalgo's army stormed the town. However, the wealthy Guanajuatenses had holed up in the *Alhóndiga* with supplies and all of their possessions to wait it out, and soldiers from the Guanajuato garrison were stationed on the roof of the windowless building to protect them.

They probably would have been able to last if the large wooden door of the granary had not been burned down. According to written history, an Indian named Pípila slung one of the large paving stones on his back to protect himself from the bullets of the soldiers on the roof of the Alhóndiga, and was able to put a torch to the one door of the building. Then the Indian army rushed the building, killing all but one

The Bajío 135

of the trapped Spaniards. Once, when I was visiting with some local people in Guanajuato, a professor at the university told me that the legend of Pipila was untrue. The Spaniards, he said, had had a cannon in the building and, in their nervousness, shot out the door by mistake. Whatever the truth of the door, the massacre in the *Alhóndiga* resulted in the loss of a great deal of popular support for the revolution. Allende and Aldama were horrified it had happened, and while Hidalgo seemed to grieve over the lost lives, he also spoke in defense of his angered Indians. After this unfortunate incident, the three leaders were constantly at odds tactically. In less than six months this first stage of the revolution was over and the army had diffused. The leaders were caught, tried, and executed as traitors. And to add to the grizzly history of the *Alhóndiga,* the heads of Hidalgo, Allende, Aldama, and Jímenez (another revolutionary figure) were hung in cages from the four corners of the granary until the revolution had been won some ten years later. The *Alhóndiga* is now a museum, and a wonderful one, full of art and historical items of the country as well as examples of the arts and crafts of the Guanajuato area.

Today, Guanajuato is a tribute to its colonial past, unmarred by industry or modernization. The old, center section of the city is colonially picturesque. Guanajuato is also good for walking since it is easily possible to walk the entire length of the ravine in which the city is built. Up from the central *jardín* (or plaza) is a little restaurant where I ordered *Enchiladas Verdes.* The first time I tried this dish it was so hot that my eyes teared and my face broke in a flush. But I loved it then and I still do! Now I can eat them like one of the gang—without a noticeable gasp.

ENCHILADAS VERDES
(Green Enchiladas)

5 *chiles poblanos*
1 *chile jalapeño,* cored
    and seeded (optional)
1 can (13-ounce) green
    tomatoes (*tomatillos*),
    drained
¼ cup chopped cilantro
2 cloves garlic
Salt
1 egg, slightly beaten

1 cup heavy cream or
    crema (page 119)
3 cups cooked, shredded
    or chopped chicken
¼ cup broth or hot water
12 corn tortillas
Lard or oil for frying
½ cup sour cream or
    crema

Prepare *chiles poblanos* as directed (page 33). Put them in the blender with the *chile jalapeño* and purée. Add *tomatillos,* cilantro, and garlic and continue to purée. Salt to taste. Mix egg with cream or *crema* and blend with purée. Heat puréed mixture in a small frying pan. Meanwhile, heat chicken in broth or water and keep warm. Fry each tortilla lightly in lard or oil to soften. Dip tortilla in Purée, then fill with a little chicken and roll. Place enchiladas in an ovenproof dish and keep warm. When all the tortillas are filled and rolled, pour remaining purée over enchiladas. (Reheat if necessary—it should be hot.) Dribble sour cream or *crema* over all and serve immediately. Makes 12 enchiladas.

In the nearby village of Marfil, another home to me, I have a friend, Amada, who is an excellent cook. She has always been very helpful in explaining Mexican recipes and giving me tips on dishes that are not only popular in the *bajío,* but all over the republic. It was Amada who fixed *Carne Asada* for us one Christmas, grilled over an open fire on her patio. She included apples and zucchini in the grilling which she said were traditional in her family.

CARNE ASADA
(Grilled Meat)

2 pounds beef
  tenderloin*
1½ quarts *Refritos* (page
  93)
6 *chiles poblanos*
3 large roasting
  potatoes, halved
3 medium-sized yellow
  onions peeled and
  halved

6 tart apples, halved
  and cored
3 large zucchini, halved
  and quartered
  lengthwise
Coarse salt
Lime wedges

Slice beef diagonally (¼-inch thick). Prepare *Refritos* and keep warm. Prepare chiles as directed for *Chiles Rellenos* (page 32), then cut each chile into four strips and keep warm. Over hot coals, grill potatoes, onions, and apples first. When they are almost tender, lower grate to about 2 inches above coals and add meat strips and zucchini slices so that everything is done about the same time. Transfer to a platter and sprinkle meat with coarse salt. Add chile strips and lime wedges to platter. Set beside *Refritos* pot and allow guests to help themselves. Serves 6.

Chorizo sausage in casings may be grilled with the beef, but they should be simmered in water for 15 to 20 minutes before grilling.

Another dish Amada prepared for us one night during the same Christmas season was *Rajas de Pollo* (Strips of Chicken), a perfectly delicious cheesy dish that is served with *Arroz Blanco*. I think it has never tasted quite as good again as Amada's did, but this is often the way with the introduction to something that you like so much.

RAJAS DE POLLO
(Strips of Chicken)

1 large chicken (fryer/
roaster) with giblets
3 cups water
1 large onion, peeled and
quartered
6 to 7 *chiles poblanos*
4 corn tortillas, cut into
½-inch strips

Oil or lard
1 cup *crema* (page 119)
or heavy cream
½ pound grated soft
white cheese
(Monterey Jack or
Muenster)
Salt

Put chicken and giblets in large pot with water and onion and simmer until tender (1½ to 2 hours). Strain off broth and let cool. Let chicken cool enough to handle and remove skin and bones. Cut the chicken in strips and return to pot. Skim fat off cooled broth and add to chicken. Meanwhile, prepare *chiles poblanos* as directed (page 33) and cut them into thin strips. Fry tortilla strips crisp in hot oil or lard and add with chiles to chicken. Heat all ingredients through and just before serving, stir in *crema* or cream and cheese and heat until cheese is melted and all ingredients are hot. Salt to taste. Serve with *Arroz Blanco* (page 37). Serves 6.

There are only two good accesses to the city of Guanajuato, from the west coming through Marfil, and from the east through San Miguel de Allende. Just outside of town on the eastern road is a large motel/restaurant that overlooks the city with a panoramic view. On many a windswept night we sat drinking their delicious frothy *margaritas* while watching the sunset, purple and gold, color the hills behind Marfil.

Margaritas are probably the most popular drink in Mexico now, replacing the famous *cuba libre* of the 1930s and 1940s. *Cuba Libres* are made of rum and Coca Cola and Mexicans often drink them without ice. I cannot think of a more unappetizing combination (even with ice), and the *margarita,* by comparison, is a brilliant concoction. With each round of drinks in this pleasant airy place a tasty appetizer was served—homemade French fries with *salsa,* little balls of white cheese, peanuts with lime. . . . These snacks were a good safety valve as the road home was steep and winding.

MARGARITA

2 ounces white tequila	1 ounce Triple Sec or
1½ ounces fresh lime	Cointreau
juice	Crushed ice

In a blender put tequila, lime juice, Triple Sec or Cointreau with 4 ounces of crushed ice. Blend until frothy. Rub the rim of the glass in ice, then dip it in salt and fill with blended mixture. Makes 1 *margarita.*

Mornings in Mexico are cheerful. The country comes to life early and it's impossible not to want to join in the activity. It's also a good time for highway travel (a few less trucks and buses), especially when you are taking the road that winds through the hills east of Guanajuato. Originally, these hills were covered with madrone and oak, but now the growth is mostly low shrub, chaparral, mesquite, and some pine. Years of cutting wood for heat and cooking, for furniture and mine beams have changed the terrain but it is still a pretty drive with many nice vistas of the tranquil hills. This road, that ultimately takes us to San Miguel de Allende, straightens, once out of the protective hills around the capital. The first stop is the town of Dolores Hidalgo, the kick-off point for the famous curate and his revolutionary army. In spite of the historical significance of this area and its link to Guanajuato, the road between the two cities was not paved until 1960.

Dolores is unspoiled by tourist traffic, although it is a well-known spot for tile buying since ceramic tiles from the town are famous all over the republic. And the Hidalgo museum is a rather spare but interesting stop. It is the house where he lived and the rooms contain the original furnishings along with papers, books, vestments, and weapons from some of Hidalgo's battles. The enormous church on the plaza with its great doors framed by *churrigueresque* carvings of that time must have presented an impressive backdrop for Hidalgo as he delivered his now-famed *Grito* (shout) in the revolution against Spain. There, by torchlight, early one cold September morning 170 years ago, was the beginning of the end of Spanish imperialism in Mexico.

There is a hotel restaurant on the plaza in Dolores where we always stop as a break in the ride between San Miguel and Guanajuato. I had, for the first time in this beautifully tiled restaurant, a most refreshing drink which I think is peculiar to Mexico. *Agua de Jamaica* is a slightly acidy-fruity drink made from the dried, dark-red hibiscus blossoms. I saw the piles of blossoms in the Guanajuato market, but it was in Dolores that I discovered how to prepare them. Jamaica (another name for hibiscus) flowers are available in the United States in small packages and the drink is a nice treat on a hot day.

AGUA DE JAMAICA

(Jamaica Water)

1 ounce (approximately) Jamaica blossoms	Sugar to taste
	Lime juice to taste
1½ quarts water	Crushed ice

Put the Jamaica blossoms in a bowl and pour 2 cups cold water over them. Let this steep for 1 hour or until the water takes on a deep burgundy color. Strain out the blossoms and discard. Add remaining water and sugar and lime juice to taste. Serve over crushed ice, garnished with a lime slice. Makes 1½ quarts.

Another memorable visit to this same restaurant occurred many years ago when my son, Lee, was five years old. It was a chilly night just before Christmas, and we had been shopping during the day in San Miguel with a friend from Guanajuato and her son. The boys had become restless waiting in the car and shops, so the other lad, a couple of years older than Lee, told stories of Dracula for their amusement. By the end of the day, Lee was beginning to wear under the horror of this character and wanted to hear no more. We drove back toward home in silence but in Dolores decided to stop for a bowl of soup. After supper we started out again but were held up by a *posada* procession going by the church. *Posada* means "inn" in Spanish, and *las posadas* are the pre-Christmas celebrations depicting the search for the inn and the celebration of the birth of the Baby Jesus. Almost every home, and certainly every village or town has some *posada* celebration.

We drove slowly by the *posada* procession—a very realistic entourage with Mary and Joseph barefoot and Mary riding on a donkey, their way lit by torches. As we passed and as we continued out toward the highway, Ann, my friend, explained to Lee the reason for this celebration, embellishing it nicely for she was a good storyteller. Lee, a good listener, sat thoughtfully absorbing the story and the significance of the event, I thought. There was a long thoughtful pause from the children, and then Lee said, "Ann, what I'd like to know is what would the Baby Jesus do to Dracula?"

As for the soup we had back in Dolores, it was *Sopa de Ajo* (Garlic Soup), a delicious favorite in Mexico.

SOPA DE AJO

(Garlic Soup)

9 cloves garlic	1 sprig *epazote*
¼ cup olive oil	3 eggs
3 slices French bread, cubed	Salt
	Lime wedges
5 to 6 cups rich chicken broth	

Mince garlic and sauté in oil until golden brown. (Do not burn.) Strain garlic from oil, return oil to pan and sauté bread in oil until golden-colored. Add to this the chicken broth along with the *epazote,* cover, and simmer for 10 minutes. Remove cover; break eggs into soup and stir until they are cooked. Add salt to taste and serve soup with lime wedges. Serves 4 to 5.

San Miguel de Allende is very popular with Americans and has an enormous American colony which is evident in the first few hours. This is understandable as it is a pretty town with cobbled streets, low colonial buildings, lots of flowery gardens, and a generally active aura. San Miguel awakens early and the streets quickly fill with adults and children greeting each other on their way to work, to market, or to school. In Mexico, *adiós* means both "hello" and "goodbye," and it is the courtesy of the road to greet strangers as well as familiar faces. In the morning, on the busy little avenues of Mexican towns and villages you will hear a lilting *adiós* with the accent on the last syllable so that the "a" is almost lost.

San Miguel is friendly and I am certainly not one to scoff at the areas that attract foreigners. After all, I am one. And this is a pleasant place to live with its many shops, restaurants, cultural events, and generally good climate. The Art Institute has long been popular with foreign students and is considered quite reputable. There are other schools in San Miguel, also, including an equestrian center.

Certainly the town is peaceful now if we compare it to its torn and divided state during the revolution against Spain. Directly on the central plaza is the house that belonged to Ignazio Jose Allende, Captain of the Spanish Army Garrison in San Miguel (then called San Miguel el Grande). It was to this house that a messenger was sent from Querétaro bearing news of the Viceroy's knowledge of the impending revolution. Allende was in Dolores with Hidalgo at the time, so the messenger was sent on to Captain Juan Aldama who then rode, by horseback, the fifty miles to Dolores to warn Hidalgo and Allende.

This is all historical romance now, and San Miguel for the contemporary tourist is a lovely relaxing spot with elegant hotels and excellent restaurants. The cuisine is varied, certainly mostly Mexican, but with other influences, too. For instance, on this last visit I sat with a friend in a peaceful, tree-lined patio restaurant eating *Enchiladas Suisas* (Swiss Enchiladas). They are mild and delicious, especially good for those who have not yet acquired a taste for the hotter enchilada sauces. *Enchiladas Suisas* are made simply with tomatoes and cream. Sometimes eggs are added to the sauce.

ENCHILADAS SUISAS
(Swiss Enchiladas)

2 pounds tomatoes, peeled and chopped	Salt
1 medium onion, chopped	3 cups chopped or shredded cooked chicken
2 cloves garlic, mashed	½ cup chicken broth
1½ cups *crema* (page 119) or cream	⅛ teaspoon nutmeg
⅓ cup oil	12 corn tortillas

Put tomatoes, onions, and garlic in blender and purée. Stir in 1 cup *crema* or cream and cook purée in 3 tablespoons of the oil over medium heat until slightly thickened. Salt to taste and set aside to keep warm. In a small pan heat chicken in broth, add nutmeg and also keep warm. In a frying pan put remaining oil and fry each tortilla to soften. Dip each tortilla in the sauce, fill with a little chicken, then roll tortilla and place in a flat casserole dish. When all enchiladas are rolled, pour remaining hot tomato sauce over them, followed by the remaining *crema* or cream. Makes 12 enchiladas.

A swing down from San Miguel on the way to Querétaro will take you along the edges of Celaya, a tidy, attractive town with two major stars in its credits. It is the birthplace (and resting spot) of the respected early nineteenth centry artist/architect, Francisco Eduardo Tresguerras, who was well known for his beautifully designed churches. The other feature of Celaya concerns *cajeta,* a delicious soft caramel candy that is packaged in little wooden boxes or jars that are shipped all over the republic. *Cajeta* refers to the little boxes, the original container, and the makers insist that their candy (with the authentic kind containing goat's milk) is the best milk candy available. I agree and when I was first in Mexico I ate it on everything, and by the spoonful too. Some is flavored with wine or vanilla, but here is the way I like it.

CAJETA DE CELAYA
(Celaya Caramel Candy)

1 quart cow's milk	1½ teaspoons cornstarch
1 quart goat's milk	1 teaspoon baking soda
2 cups sugar	

Combine all but 1 cup of milk with sugar and put in a saucepan. Bring to a boil and reduce heat to a simmer. Dissolve cornstarch and soda in remaining cup of milk and stir into hot milk mixture. Cook and stir occasionally until mixture is thickened and golden brown. This takes anywhere from 1½ to 3 hours, during which time the mixture will cook down. Cool and store in covered jars. Serve on cookies, over ice cream, etc. Cooks down to approximately 1 quart.

Querétaro, capital of the state of the same name, is a charming city in every sense. It is colonial, wealthy, well-maintained, rich in churches and *jardines* (a word more common in this region and used to refer to *plazas* or *zócalos*). And it has an amazing aqueduct, built almost 250 years ago by some foresighted colonial engineers, which still carries water into the city.

Querétaro is a city with a political history. It was here that Maximilian hid until he was executed by Benito Juárez above the town on El Cerro de las Campanas (The Hill of the Bells). Yet, it was also here that the revolutionary figures, including Hidalgo, met under the guise of being a literary society. In 1848, the Treaty of Guadalupe was signed in Querétaro, a major property loss for Mexico after the defeat of General Santa Ana the year before. Under the terms of this treaty, Mexico lost nearly 900,000 square miles of territory to the United States—a considerable change in boundary.

Remnants of these and other historical events are on display in the regional museum of Querétaro. One of these is the printing press that turned out the Mexican constitution of 1917 which is still in effect today. President Venustiano Carranza and General Alvaro Obregón are credited with originating this most sensible and socially modern document. It gave subsoil rights to the country, the basis for the later nationalization of oil. It also called for stringent reform in the labor laws, limited the clergy's right to hold property, and required compulsory education in primary, secular schools. Because Mexico was a nation governed by the Church, this was not a popular constitution at the time.

Although the Querétaro of today is modern, high-paced and industrial, it still carries all the features of a colonial town—the beauty, elegance, ritual, and festivity that is so much a part of old Mexico. It was in Querétaro that I tried the traditional *Pan de Muerte* (Bread of the Dead) baked for All Souls Day in early November. On this day Mexican families visit the graves of the deceased in their families and celebrate the eternity of their souls by making a picnic of the visits. On Janitzio, the little island in Lake Pátzcuaro, and in Oaxaca, these festivities are greatly honored and in nearly every town and village you will see special foods, candy skulls, and various food souvenirs made especially for the day. Bread of the Dead, a kind of coffee cake, is traditional fare and is usually decorated with dough in the shapes of crosses, tears, and bones.

PAN DE MUERTE
(Bread of the Dead)

1 package dry yeast	1 tablespoon grated
½ cup lukewarm water	orange rind
5 cups flour	1½ cups confectioners
1 teaspoon salt	sugar
¾ cup sugar	1 teaspoon vanilla
1 cup butter, melted	Milk
and cooled	Pink sugar crystals
6 eggs, lightly beaten	
2 tablespoons anise	
water*	
2 tablespoons orange	
blossom water	
(available in gourmet	
shops)	

Dissolve yeast in water and add 1 cup of the flour. Stir to make a soft sponge, cover with a cloth, and let rise in a warm place until doubled in bulk. Set aside ½ cup flour. To the yeast mixture, add the rest of the flour mixed with salt and sugar, and the cooled butter that has been mixed with eggs, anise water, orange blossom water, and orange rind. Mix well and turn out on a board floured with remaining ½ cup flour. Dough will be soft so keep hands floured and knead lightly. Pat into a greased bowl and set in a warm place for about 1½ hours to rise. Shape into round loaf—it helps to have a round baking pan for support. (Traditionally, a little dough is used to decorate the top of each loaf with crosses, tears, and bones. These shapes are allowed to rise with the loaf and attached just before baking.) Bake in preheated 350° oven for about 30 minutes. Cool and frost with confectioners sugar mixed with vanilla and only enough milk to make a glaze of frosting consistency (only the top is frosted). Sprinkle with pink sugar crystals. Makes 1 loaf.

*To make anise water put 1 tablespoon anise seeds in ¼ cup water and simmer for 3 to 4 minutes. Let steep 10 minutes and then strain off seeds.

While in Querétaro a trip through the wine country is a must. It's hard to incorporate in a vision of Mexican life, past or present, an afternoon of wine tasting, yet it is possible. And even though negative comments are made about the quality of Mexican wines there are some very good ones available.

A little south of the city of Querétaro, on the toll road, is San Juan del Rio, known principally for being a gem city, especially opals which come from the nearby mines. Other gems are also imported into this area as it seems to be a place to find many semi-precious stones. (Stick to the shops, though, and avoid "hot deals" on the street.) It is on the road to Tequisquiapan, an attractive little town, also selling stones and a lot of wicker goods, that you will find the *bodegas* (literally "wine cellars"— meaning wineries).

There is a law against wine tasting (perhaps a local law), but in Mexico such laws are often ignored. On an earlier ride, my niece and I stopped in two wineries that were more or less set up for tasting and the proprietors were most cordial. We came away that afternoon feeling warm and relaxed, with a few bottles of very nice wine under our arms.

CHAPTER EIGHT

The Southern West Coast

PUERTO ESCONDIDO

I CONFESS a preference for the western coast of Mexico. It may be because I am from the western side of the continent and I like the sun to set over the water, and I love a mild climate (although there are occasional earthquakes and hurricanes on this side). I know that Tampico is an interesting city—a tropical point in time, and Veracruz is very beautiful, but there is nothing quite comparable to the sunsets seen from the cliffs of Acapulco, the small-town friendliness of Zihuatanejo, and Ixtapa's graceful long beaches. Even the hubbub of Manzanillo's port is offset by the tropical fruit plantations and the wonderful warm snorkeling water. And what can ever match the rocky southern coves of Puerta Vallarta with the swirling blue-green tides and warm breezes? Further north are Mazatlán and Guaymas, busy seaside resorts only a few hours by air from the western United States. The only drawback for me on the west coast is that the western highway, Route 15, does not run the entire length of the upper coast and along the lower coast, does not hug the water clear through to Guatemala. But I really can't quarrel with the impossible.

A good start toward exploring this area is to take one of the roads from Oaxaca through the mountains to the coast—either to Puerto Ángel, or to Puerto Escondido. Both are sleepy fishing villages being courted by developers, although it appears that Puerto Escondido is getting the bigger rush. We took the road to Puerto Escondido and I understand it is not unlike the one to Puerto Ángel—narrow, rutted, unpaved, and practically devoid of traffic. The mountains are rugged and covered with tall timber and brush which becomes more tropical as you near the water. When we stopped to ask if we were still on the main road to the coast (it's not easy to tell as the road looks like a fire break) it seemed as though the Indians in the area did not want to speak Spanish. There were a number of settlements along the way, and we were told later that this is potentially a revolutionary area. Perhaps that explains the large poster we saw of Che Guevara on one of the small hillside houses.

Puerto Escondido, meaning hidden port, is as quiet as its name (or was, at least). There were a couple of marginal-looking hotels and a couple of rather nice-looking ones. We were pleased with the one we selected and after that long ride (eight hours for only a hundred miles) it was relaxing to sit on the patio, overlooking the coastline, sipping the rich, dark *Añejo* rum over ice. *Añejo* means "old," and with lime and ice it is one of the great *bebidas* (drinks) of the coast. The village of Puerto Escondido is small, the main street unpaved but it has several lively little family restaurants. Naturally, the fish is fresh in terms of minutes here, and we had *Huachinango con Ajo* (Red Snapper with Garlic) which was unforgettable, especially served with *Papas Fritas* (Fried Potatoes), and sliced tomatoes.

HUACHINANGO CON AJO
(Red Snapper with Garlic)

4 large snapper fillets	Salt and pepper
16 cloves garlic	Sliced tomatoes
Lime	
Olive oil	

Allow 4 garlic cloves for each fillet. Mince garlic carefully and stud both sides of the fillets, pressing the garlic into the flesh. Squeeze lime over 1 side of the fillets and brush same side lightly with olive oil. Place oiled side of fish on a grill and cook about 4 inches above hot coals. When fish begins to flake on the underside and develops some grill marks, turn and repeat process with lime and olive oil. Salt and pepper lightly, cover fish with sliced tomatoes, and serve accompanied by lime wedges and *Papas Fritas.* Serves 4.

PAPAS FRITAS

(Fried Potatoes)

1 large yellow onion, peeled, quartered and sliced	2 pounds red-skinned potatoes, cubed but unpeeled
5 tablespoons oil	Salt, pepper, lime

Sauté onions in 2 tablespoons oil until just beginning to turn translucent; then add remaining oil and potatoes. Fry the potatoes over a high-medium heat until browned, but not mushy, stirring frequently to keep them from sticking to the pan. Salt and pepper to taste. Squeeze some lime juice over them before serving. Serves 4.

Puerto Escondido is best as a starting point north in the fall, winter, or spring. (It gets very hot in the summer.) You can't help but develop a love of the landscape that is so beautifully repeated in the following five hundred miles of coastline—thick groves of coconut palms, calm rivers, silent lagoons, uncom-

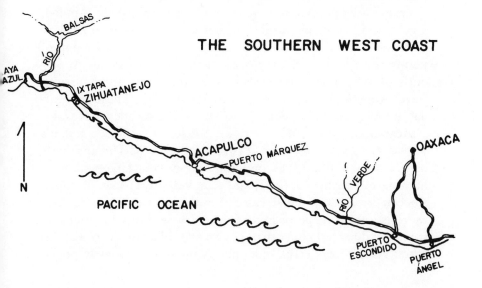

THE SOUTHERN WEST COAST

The Southern West Coast 153

monly clear and warm water, and a generally easy way of life. As a people, Mexicans are unimpressed with time schedules or deadlines, and they seem even more so in the sunny, humid coastal areas. This leisurely attitude can be very frustrating to the punctually oriented or to someone who is trying to make a transportation connection. But when you are vacationing, especially in the tropics, the slow and easy pace is perfect medicine for the harried soul.

Driving north toward Acapulco the road is good; it cuts through more of the same palm and beach area, although the ocean is not continually visible from the highway. There are a number of lagoons and fishing is one of the major means of livelihood here. The dramatic water confrontation is with the Rió Verde river. There are a few other bridge crossings on this stretch of road, but the bridge over the Rió Verde, used in the dry season, is special. It is made of palm poles and washes away each year when the rains come—and is rebuilt again the next season. (A ferry takes over during the rainy season.) The poles of the bridge run parallel with the car and I worried that our wheels were going to become trapped between the poles. But they didn't, and it seems that any and every vehicle makes it across without getting stuck.

Frequently, people in these tropical areas are darker skinned, a genetic adjustment to the sun, but a little more than halfway between Puerto Escondido and Acapulco is a settlement of people who look as if they come from the Caribbean. Apparently, during Acapulco's earlier, busy, port days, some African slaves were able to get away and traveled south. These present-day people are descendents of some of the escaped slaves.

Acapulco is the "in" resort of Mexico, of course, and it's necessary to see it for what it is to appreciate it. The antithesis of places like Puerto Escondido, Acapulco is large, modern, high-paced, flashy, touristic, and relatively expensive, although since it is also a popular resort for the Mexican middle class there is a wide range of hotel prices. I love Acapulco, but that is mainly due to the fact that we discovered some years ago, on a first visit, a wonderful, old, and lovely hotel, modestly-priced and sitting on a cliff above the Pacific. Most of the rooms have balconies with hammocks hung facing the sea. There is also a small veranda for the sunset-watching hour, and an open-air restaurant and pool, also perched on the cliff. Who wouldn't be loyal to a place like that? Here, as we watched those spectacular late afternoon colors we ate peanuts and drank Tequila Sunrises. This drink is made in several different ways, but this is the way I like it.

TEQUILA SUNRISE

2 teaspoons grenadine
Crushed ice
2 ounces white tequila

4 ounces fresh orange
juice
Sparkling water

In a tall, chilled glass pour grenadine over crushed ice. Mix together tequila and orange juice and pour over grenadine. Fill the glass with sparkling water and stir lightly without disturbing the grenadine for it is supposed to look like a sunrise. Makes 1 drink.

Acapulco means "place where the reeds grow," and it was first settled in the 1530s. Its bay and the smaller one at Puerto Marquez, a little south, were both fine natural harbors for Cortés's ships that were sent to raid the Philippines. Eventually, vessels were based there for trade with the East—silks and spices for silver. The cargo was then sent overland to Veracruz to be shipped to Spain. (It was in Acapulco, too, that Pizarro outfitted his ships for the conquest of Peru.) Naturally, with so much action, and so many valuable goods going in and out of the harbor, there was a problem with English and Dutch pirates (one devil of notoriety was Sir Francis Drake). To protect the waterway, a fort, El Castillo de San Diego, was built on a hill overlooking the harbor. An earthquake took it down at the end of the eighteenth century, but it was eventually rebuilt and now serves as a museum.

In the early nineteenth century, Mexico's break from Spain made the port no longer that important, and the expansion in other areas of the country was of more interest to the government. It wasn't until the 1920s that the town began to acquire resort status, and it really did not become popular with foreigners until the 1950s when the great developing began. Acapulco is a major international resort spot now and in the main section, all the beaches are crowded. (Most of the hotels have pools, too.) However, there are still some relatively deserted beach fronts to the north and south of the city.

Acapulco is a real city, and there is much to do if you wish to leave the beach or pool side. It is, to say the least, heavy in night life with everything from contemporary disco dancing to Mexican folk music—those beautiful melodies played on the guitar, their mournful lyrics sung by haunting male voices. One of the biggest night attractions in Acapulco is the *Quebrada* divers by the *El Mirador Hotel.* Although Mexico is not known for taking medals in Olympic diving, these extraordinary young men dive every night from the high cliffs by the hotel into a narrow channel between the rocks below. The only time a dive is safe is when each wave washes in, so the divers have to have a perfect sense of timing. They don't seem to have accidents, perhaps because they never fail to offer a prayer to the Virgin at the shrine in the rocks. These divers are a very strong tourist attraction and quite a spectacular one. I don't necessarily recommend dining in the hotel, though.

Tennis, golf, jai alai, bullfighting, shopping, drinking, and eating are the major tourist occupations in Acapulco. The eating is wonderful and there are many good restaurants specializing in both grilled meats and fish. My brother, a connoisseur of prawns, had a terrific dish of cold marinated prawns here. Imagine, if you will, a warm but breezy night, with the lights of Acapulco reflected in the quiet bay while you systematically move through a plate of chilled, fresh large prawns with a side dish of sliced tomatoes covered with *guacamole,* accompanied by a very cold beer.

CAMARONES EN FRIO

(Cold, Marinated Prawns)

⅓ cup lime juice
2 large, mild onions,
  thinly sliced
1 cup oil
1½ to 2 pounds fresh
  prawns (about 30),
  unshelled
Coarse salt
3 tablespoons lime juice
3 tablespoons white
  wine vinegar

4 large cloves garlic,
  minced
2 tablespoons minced
  cilantro
1 teaspoon prepared
  mustard
2 tablespoons minced,
  pickled (*en escabeche*)
  chile jalapeño

Pour lime juice over onions, let sit for 1 hour, then sauté in ¼ cup of the oil until onions are soft and clear. Remove onions from pan and add ¼ cup more oil and sauté prawns, unshelled, salting them as they turn pink. When the prawns are pink remove from pan and mix with onions and cool slightly. Mix together remaining ingredients and pour over cooled prawns and onions. Toss lightly and chill well. Serve on lettuce leaves. Serves 4.

GUACAMOLE

3 ripe avocados
⅓ cup minced onion
1 clove garlic, mashed
1 tomato, peeled and
  diced (optional)
2 tablespoons chopped
  cilantro

1 tablespoon lime or
  lemon juice
Hot pepper sauce
Salt

Halve avocados and remove seeds. Scoop out flesh and mash until smooth. Add onion, garlic, tomato if desired, cilantro, and lime or lemon juice and mix well. Add hot pepper sauce and salt to taste. Makes about 2 cups.

Do not make too far in advance of eating. Avocado mixture will stay greener if you keep one of the pits in the *guacamole* until it is served.

The tropical fruit and citrus smells also distinguish Mexico's west coast. Limes are cheap and abundant and are used much more liberally in cooking than Americans use lemons. (As I mentioned before, Mexicans squeeze lime on everything from meat to beer.) I love the smell and taste of lime juice, although I suggest lemons when limes are just not available. I do think lime is irreplaceable in some dishes and I would buy the unreconstituted, unsweetened bottled lime juice rather than using lemon juice. For instance, this delicious mango dessert we had in Acapulco is best with lime juice. You can use canned mangoes, but be careful not to use the variety that is sold in Asian markets because they are very stringy.

POSTRE DE MANGO
(Mango Dessert)

2 tablespoons gelatin	2 cups cream or *crema*
¼ cup warm water	½ cup sour cream
3 cups fresh or canned	½ cup lime juice
(drained) mango pulp	Honey to taste

Dissolve gelatin in warm water and cook over a low heat until clear. Put in blender with mangoes, cream or *crema,* sour cream, and lime juice. Blend until smooth and add honey to taste. (I prefer this with very little added sweetening because mangoes are very sweet.) Pour into a serving bowl or dessert dishes and chill. Serves 6.

Not much of the ocean can be seen on the road from Acapulco north to Zihuatanejo since all along the coastline are coconut plantations. This is a big copra-producing area (dried coconut meat, from which coconut oil is extracted). The road is modern, but there is an undisturbed quality about the small settlements along the way. It's a relaxing drive with a pleasant destination.

Zihuatanejo is an attractive, low-keyed fishing village, as well as a thoroughly Mexican old-beach resort that is built around a sparkling little bay, perfect for swimming and snorkeling. Ixtapa, just a few miles north, is a developer's dream— a long line of new luxury highrise hotels, not at all Mexican, but built on one of the loveliest, cleanest, sandy beaches of the coast. It reminded me a bit of the long beaches of "old" southern California. I understand this section of Ixtapa gets posted occasionally for dangerous surf, but it was serene and unmarked when we were there.

Zihuatanejo is by far the more interesting spot. It's a real town with shops and restaurants, and fairly modest but charming hotels which circle the bay. The town is growing, but the style is being preserved (tidy whitewashed buildings with tile roofs) by government intention. They insist that the new jetport at Ixtapa will not change the face of Zihuatanejo, and that they are *not* pushing for another Acapulco. It's still pretty slow-paced at this writing and there are several very informal restaurants in the town that specialize in the fish from the bay.

Ceviche, the famed marinated raw fish dish of Spanish-speaking countries, is a specialty of Zihuatanejo cuisine. Mexicans prefer a fatty fish, generally mackerel, but red snapper is also acceptable or even a not-too-delicate sole. Don't blanch at the idea of eating raw fish because the lime juice cooks it as well as if it had been cooked over a fire. This dish is generally used as a first course or as an appetizer, but I can make a meal of it.

Lemon juice can be used in this recipe because, as a citrus fruit, it will also cook the meat but lime is much better.

CEVICHE
(Marinated Raw Fish)

2 pounds fish, cut into bite-sized pieces
1½ cups lime or lemon juice
1 medium white onion, peeled and chopped
2 medium tomatoes, cored and chopped
2 canned pickled (*en escabeche*) *chiles jalapeños,* minced
¼ cup olive oil
2 tablespoons chopped cilantro
½ teaspoon oregano
Salt and pepper to taste

Cover fish with lime or lemon juice and marinate for about 6 hours, stirring a couple of times during this time (The fish should develop a cooked opaque look.) After marinating, toss fish with other ingredients, chill ½ hour, and serve on lettuce leaves. Serves 6 as a first course.

Mexico is not really a salad eating country as we are—or have become. (In the resort areas however, there is now more of a reflection of our restaurant menus.) But they do use raw vegetables on hot dishes as garnishes—shredded lettuce, cabbage or carrots, sliced radishes and chopped tomatoes on enchiladas, with tostadas, soups, etc. Often, grilled meat or fish will be accompanied on the plate by a little shredded cabbage and onion sprinkled with lime juice or white vinegar. But there is one salad you often see on a menu, *Ensalada Mixta* (Mixed Salad). This can be many combinations of vegetables that are usually slightly steamed, chopped small, and lightly dressed. In Zihuatanejo we had a salad of this type that was heavy in cilantro, a taste that I favor.

ENSALADA MIXTA

(Mixed Salad)

2 cooked red-skinned potatoes
2 medium carrots, lightly steamed
½ pound fresh green beans, lightly steamed
2 cups cauliflower flowerets, lightly steamed
1 medium zucchini, lightly steamed
1 small cucumber, peeled
1 bunch scallions
3 tablespoons chopped cilantro
Vinaigrette dressing
Salt and pepper
Lime wedges

Chop all vegetables the same size (in about ½-inch cubes). Add cilantro and toss lightly with vinaigrette dressing and salt and pepper to taste. Chill well and serve with lime wedges. Serves 4.

VINAIGRETTE DRESSING

½ cup safflower oil
⅓ cup olive oil
½ cup white wine vinegar
2 cloves garlic, mashed
2 teaspoons mayonnaise
½ teaspoon each thyme, Dijon-style mustard, and brown sugar
½ teaspoon salt
Ground black pepper

In blender or in a jar with a lid put oils, vinegar, garlic, mayonnaise, thyme, mustard, sugar and salt. Blend or shake until well mixed. Add a little ground black pepper. Makes about 1½ cups.

It's a rather short, but scenic ride from Zihuatanejo to Playa Azul, passing through more sleepy settlements, coconut groves, gentle streams and with views of the majestic Sierra Madre del

Sur Mountains to the east. There is one big, and impressive river on this route, the Rió Balsas, and the highway passes right over a recently built dam. The little town of Playa Azul is the quietest yet on this route, and still primarily a beach town. When Highway 200, which now ends at Playa Azul, is finally finished and connects with Manzanillo and the northern Pacific ports, Playa Azul will surely (perhaps sadly) grow, too.

On our last trip though the republic we kept asking if the road from Playa Azul to Manzanillo had been completed and everyone said "yes"—or, at least they thought so. (Since it had not, this was a truly Mexican piece of travel information.) Believing what we heard, and starting down the road, our faces fell when the blacktop turned into dirt. The unavoidable jog was made by going back into the interior and then going through Uruapan, Jiquilpan, and back down to the coast again through Cuidad Guzmán, and Colima. It's a nice route, but a bit of a disappointment when you are counting on clinging to the coastline.

While we were in Playa Azul, a nice stop really, with its wide sandy beaches and good waves for swimming, we stopped for a beer and a snack in a pleasant hotel restaurant with a nice view. We had a chilled avocado soup accompanied by *bolillos* and from what I could understand it was made more or less in the following way.

SOPA DE AGUACATE
(Avocado Soup)

3 large avocados
3 cups chicken broth
2 tablespoons grated onion
¼ cup medium-dry sherry

Salt and pepper
1½ cups *crema* or heavy cream

Mash avocado flesh and put in blender with a little of the chicken broth and blend until smooth. Combine with remaining chicken broth and onions. Heat over a low flame until tastes combine well. (Do not allow mixture to get overly hot.) Add sherry, and salt and pepper to taste. Remove from heat and slowly stir in the *crema* or heavy cream. Chill soup well and serve with lime wedges.

CHAPTER NINE

The Central West Coast

MAZATLÁN

*B*ACK on the Pacific coast, after our enforced swing through the interior, our destination was the port city of Manzanillo, beautifully set against tropical mountains, and amidst coconut palm and banana groves. This is a recent resort area of the international set, partly due to the popularity of the very elegant resort, Las Hadas, just north of Manzanillo. This Arabian-like delight, built by a Bolivian tin magnate and now controlled by other money, is a complex unto itself. (It has its own electric cars for transportation within the compound.) But it reflects little of the style of old (or new) Manzanillo.

Way back in the days of Cortés, Manzanillo was an active port—a stop for the loaded Spanish galleons returning from the Philippines. It's a deep natural harbor and still very active in shipping out bananas, copra, hardwood, and coffee. Also, because of the rail connections to the interior, Manzanillo acts as a receiving port for a wide variety of imports which are then shipped all over Mexico.

The city strings out along the water with modest hotels and swimming beaches. Food is good in Manzanillo particularly if you are a fish lover as the waters around yield a great variety of catch. I had red snapper in a parsley sauce (*Huachinango en Salsa Perejil*) that was wonderful, in part because the snapper was incomparably fresh. This recipe is easy enough to make with canned green tomatoes (*tomatillos*).

167

HUACHINANGO EN SALSA PEREJIL

(Red Snapper in Parsley Sauce)

1 can (13-ounce) green
   tomatoes (*tomatillos*)
1 small onion, finely
   chopped
2 cloves garlic, mashed
2 cups parsley, loosely
   packed

2 tablespoons lime or
   lemon juice
1 scant teaspoon salt
4 large snapper fillets
Lime wedges
Pickled (*en escabeche*) *chiles
jalapeños*

Drain green tomatoes and blend smooth. Transfer to a bowl and mix with onions, garlic, parsley, and lime or lemon juice. Add salt to taste. Lay fish in a shallow baking pan. Heat parsley sauce and pour over fish. Bake, uncovered, in a hot (475°) oven for about 10 minutes or until fish flakes easily with fork. Serve with lime wedges, chiles, and *Arroz Blanco* (page 37). Serves 4.

In Manzanillo, I had my first experience with a Piña Colada, the newer, more popular drink of the west coast. Served in big, frosty glasses, this drink is for all seasons.

PIÑA COLADA

3 ounces coconut milk
3 ounces pineapple juice
3 ounces light rum

Crushed ice
Fresh pineapple slice

In the blender put all ingredients except the pineapple slice. Blend until frothy and pour into a chilled glass. Put the piece of pineapple over the rim of the glass for garnish. Makes 1 drink.

The road that links Manzanillo with Puerto Vallarta is paved now, and an easy day's drive even with a rest stop at Barra de

Navidad (also a good place to stay overnight). There are a
number of beaches north of Manzanillo that are fairly deserted
and very desirable to surfers and sunbathers. North of Barra
the highway is intersected by side roads to lagoons and small
villages to make it a leisurely and interesting drive—as long as
it is not the rainy season and you have a sturdy vehicle. Several
bridges had to be built when making this road and that is why
it took so long to string these coastal resorts together. (I once
took the road from Puerto Vallarta to Manzanillo when much
of it was gravel. It was an arduous trip, even though it wasn't
raining and we had allowed ourselves a lot of time.)

Barra de Navidad and its interesting name came about when

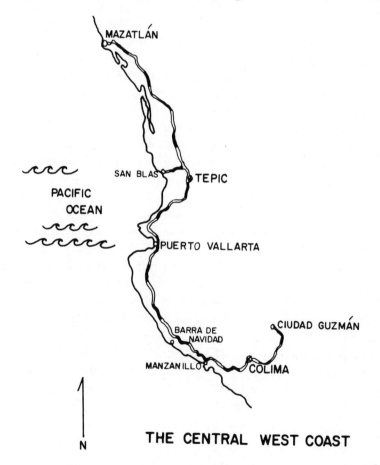

THE CENTRAL WEST COAST

the Spaniards landed on the sandbar (*barra*) that separates the ocean from the little fishing lagoon behind it. They arrived on Christmas Day—thus the addition of *Navidad.* For some time, a good road from Guadalajara has connected with Melaque Bay. Barra is located on the south end of the bay and the little village of San Patricio is at the north end, and people from the interior of Jalisco have long used this area for vacations. Fortunately, it is not spoiled or heavily developed even though it is extremely pretty all along the circle of the bay. The area seems to appeal to the budget-minded, and attracts many Americans who like to live out of their vans or buses.

It's Puerto Vallarta, farther north, that has felt the tourist boom most heavily, and in the last fifteen years it has become one of the most popular winter resorts in Mexico. Inclined to be a little less humid than Acapulco (although buggier in the summer), Puerto Vallarta is acessible both by auto and plane. Until the mid 1960s this was just a little fishing village, and, in fact, it's still a fishing center, although more of a headquarters for tourist fishing excursions.

The first time I visited Puerto Vallarta was about eight years ago during *Semana Santa,* the Easter week vacation. It was an inappropriate time to visit any Mexican resort for the first time and this particular vacation is a big holiday for civil servants. Everyone who worked for any department in the state of Jalisco or Nayarit was in Puerto Vallarta and the place was a madhouse of activity—a little like beach towns in the United States over the 4th of July.

Red snapper is probably the most popular coastal fish and it is grilled over open fires in many different ways. On the beach of Puerto Vallarta, a small snapper is skewered on a long stick, grilled, and then eaten off the stick with lime. It's a delicious way to get the full flavor because the fish is so fresh. We also had snapper baked in a garlic and citrus sauce—equally *sabroso.* In my opinion fish and garlic are the perfect culinary couple.

HUACHINANGO EN SALSA FRUTA Y AJO
(Red Snapper in Fruit and Garlic Sauce)

1 2½-pound fresh, cleaned red snapper	2 tablespoons minced cilantro
¼ cup olive oil	1 cup fresh orange juice mixed with 2 tablespoons lime juice
8 cloves garlic, minced	
½ small onion, thinly sliced	2 strips of bacon
½ green pepper, thinly sliced	Salt

Heat oil and sauté garlic, onion, and green pepper until softened and garlic is golden. (It should not be brown.) Mix with cilantro. Place fish in a baking dish and spread ½ of the mixture on the inside of the fish. Pour ⅓ cup of juice over this. Pour another ⅓ cup of the juice over the top of the fish and marinate for about 3 hours in the refrigerator. Then put 1 slice of bacon in the inside of the fish and salt lightly. Put the other slice of bacon on the top of the fish which has been covered with remaining garlic mixture and remaining juice. Salt lightly and bake in a hot oven (375°) until fish flakes easily with a fork and is no longer translucent (about 15 minutes per inch of thickness). Serves 4.

There was a time not long ago when Puerto Vallarta was only accessible by air during the rainy season as the old road connecting it to Tepic and Highway 15 would be flooded. It's not hard to imagine this because the area around the city is so verdant from the heavy rainfall. The Sierra Madre Mountain area, which separates the coast from the rest of the state, still produces exports like hardwoods and chicle, and supports a large variety of wild game. On the southern end of the city the mountains tumble into the lush coves of blue-green water. I always think of Puerto Vallarta as a tropical Big Sur as much of it has that same spectacular beauty from the road.

The beaches on the north end of Puerto Vallarta are longer, wider, and better for swimming, although water sports are popular all along Bahía de Banderas (the Bay of Flags) which is what this scoop in the coastline is called. Two of the most popular excursions for vacationers are the boat trips to the hidden beaches of Mismaloya and Yelapa (where *The Night of the Iguana* was filmed). Both of these beaches are south of the city, and although it is possible to drive to Mismaloya, the boat ride is more fun.

Puerto Vallarta is the exotic drink capital of Mexico, and though I am not inclined toward this kind of thirst quencher, I did order a *Coco Loco* the last time I was there. It was served in a large coconut shell, and had enough rum and tequila in it to scuttle a Spanish galleon (I had to share it). The weight of the drink, the coconut shell, AND the fruit on top had the waiter staggering. It's sort of a silly drink, but quite impressive and certainly appropriate for certain moods and indulgent ambiance.

COCO LOCO

1 large fresh coconut*
1½ ounces light tequila
1 ounce light rum
1 ounce Meyers rum
    (dark Jamaican rum)
½ ounce Kahlua
3½ ounces coconut milk
3½ ounces pineapple
    juice
6 ounces crushed ice
151-proof rum
1 pineapple slice
1 maraschino cherry
2 lime wedges

With a heavy knife crack the top of the coconut shell and drain out milk. Then cut off the top of the coconut as you would cut off the top of a pumpkin for a jack-o-lantern. (You need a machete-type knife for this and one good whack—so be careful.) In a blender put tequila, light rum, dark rum, Kahlua, fruit juices, and crushed ice. Blend until frothy and pour into the coconut shell. Pour a small float of 151-proof rum over the top of the drink. ("Float" is a bartender's term for a small top-off of strong liquor.) Skewer the pieces of fruit and stick end of

*If you do not have access to a fresh coconut use a large compote-type glass as a container and chill before serving.

skewer into the coconut. Serve with straws. Serves 2 persons.

One dish I just adore for breakfast in Mexico—or anywhere for that matter—is *Chilaquiles,* a kid of hash made primarily of stale tortillas, cream and cheese. It has several variations—sometimes red chiles and *chorizo* are added, sometimes green chiles and shredded chicken. Or it can be made with eggs or fish—whatever is on hand since it is primarily a way of using up old tortillas. In Puerto Vallarta I had *Chilaquiles* made with a green sauce. They were so good I ate an enormous platter-ful, much to the surprise of the waiter since they are so rich.

CHILAQUILES
(Tortilla Hash)

2 dozen stale tortillas	2½ cups grated white
Chicken fat or lard	cheese (Monterey
2 cups *Salsa Verde* (page	Jack or Muenster)
79)	1½ cup *crema* (page 119)
1 cup chicken broth	Salt to taste

Cut tortillas in ½-inch strips and fry them in hot fat or lard (about 4 tortillas at a time in ¼-inch fat). Do not let them get crisp; they should be chewy. Drain on paper towels. When all tortillas are fried, remove any remaining fat from pan and add *salsa* and broth to heat. Stir in tortilla strips, cheese, and *crema* to make a soupy hash. Add more *crema* or broth if mixture is not moist. (This should be eaten with a fork, but it should not be dry.) Salt to taste—it may not be necessary if the broth and *salsa* are well salted. Spoon *Chilaquiles* into small shallow bowls and place under the broiler just long enough for mixture to bubble. Serve immediately. Serves 6.

A couple of driving hours to the north of Puerto Vallarta, we intersected with Highway 15 at Tepic, the capital of the state of Nayarit. Just before this point is the town of Compostela from which Francisco Coronado set off to find the golden cities of Cibolá, alleged to be in the area of present-day New Mexico. The expedition was a monumental investment (and failure—no such cities), second only in size to Cortés's expedition. In this part of Mexico you will find that the historical emphasis is on the northern and northwestern expansion of New Spain into the area that is now the southwestern United States. In fact, both Father Serra and Father Kino, the California mission *padres,* lived in Tepic before starting off on their treks to convert the Indians.

Nayarit state, as a whole, is fascinating Indian country, and the city of Tepic is the market spot for the Huichol and Cora Indians who live in the nearby mountains. These creative and colorful people have difficulty maintaining a low profile when they do come into town because they dress so grandly—especially the Huichols with their hats with feathers and brightly colored ribbons, and their embroidered shirts and belts. Some of their work, like bright yarn paintings, are sold as tourist items, but socially these Indians are quite separate from other Mexicans. Few outsiders visit their villages, or are allowed to see much of their lives. For the most part, they continue to live as they always have (except for the plane rides into Tepic), and each year they take a long religious walk across the country to the old ghost town area of Real de Catorce in the state of San Luis Potosí. As part of their rituals, they eat the hallucinogenic cactus button called *peyote,* a practice they have continued for generations.

Anyone who has traveled down the western Highway 15 toward Guadalajara has been through Tepic. I don't know how many times I have stayed in this town and in how many motels, but I like it. There is a funny old park on the main road that slants in an odd way and is across from a favorite restaurant. It had changed some since the last time I visited but the decor is always a great reminder of Hollywood in the 1940s. In Tepic, I had a dish—a first for me—named *Enchiladas Sincronizadas* (Synchronized Enchiladas) and I think I ordered it for the name. It was terrific, and I suspect designed for Americans.

Anyone who has access to flour tortillas and avocados can make it. Just guess from its name how it looked.

ENCHILADAS SINCRONIZADAS
(Synchronized Enchiladas)

4 flour tortillas
Oil
2½ cups grated white
cheese (Monterey
Jack or Muenster)
2 slices ham (room
temperature or
warmed slightly)
Sliced meat from ½
chicken breast (room
temperature or
warmed slightly)
1 small tomato, thinly
sliced (room
temperature)
½ cup *Guacamole* (page
157) (room
temperature)
½ cup *crema* (page 119)
(room temperature)

Fry 3 tortillas slightly crisp in oil and spread with cheese. Put the tortillas under the broiler to melt the cheese while frying the fourth tortilla. Remove tortillas from the broiler and place the ham on the first one, then lay the second tortilla over this and cover with chicken. Follow with the third cheese tortilla and spread tomatoes over this. Top with the fourth tortilla and spread with the *Guacamole* that has been mixed with the *crema* or sour cream. (This sandwich is served warm, not hot, and the ingredients should be slightly warm.) Serve with a knife and fork. Serves 1 or 2 depending on appetite.

The drive from Tepic to Mazatlán is a breeze—even with a stop in San Blas, a top surfing spot on the western Mexican coast. San Blas, like Barra de Navidad, has changed little over the years and attracts the budget-minded who love the region for its good fishing, swimming, and surfing. This was also a Spanish port, and remnants of its heyday can still be seen near the waterfront. It's a totally unpretentious little town with a lot of youthful action, one very good hotel and a couple of very modest ones. But it seems that San Blas hosts the summer mosquito and gnat conventions of western Mexico, so if that is one of your worries it's best to visit during the winter months—November to May. This insect problem is more pronounced here than in other resort areas—partly because San Blas is such a sheltered little bay and does not seem to get as many free breezes to drive back the bugs. Also the mangroves and other tropical foliage grow so thick and close to the water along this part of the coast and this provides good breeding conditions.

The road into San Blas truly cuts through a jungle. Once, some years ago, two friends and I took the bus from Mazatlán to Tepic where we were going to catch another bus to San Blas and spend a few days. Unfortunately, the buses to San Blas were not running and there was no assurance of when they would. We decided to splurge a bit and take one of the eager taxis waiting outside the bus station. (Actually, taxis are cheap in Mexico.) So we drove through the jungle at night in a taxi to San Blas—a double anacronism. I guess it was just as well that we did not have the light of day as the driver drove like a madman, and we all held our breath and huddled in the back seat until our safe arrival.

Mazatlán is known intimately to many people in the western United States because it's such a quick trip by plane. It is a good, reasonable beach and shopping vacation spot, and though it continues to grow, it still has that small-town resort feeling. On my first visit to Mazatlán some fifteen years ago we stayed at the wonderful old Belmar Hotel in a seaside room. It was early November and we left the French doors open to the balcony. The wind blew gently all night, tossing the curtains and moving the ceiling fan—one of those hand-pulled types popular in Humphrey Bogart movies. The front rooms all had balconies and we dragged out the heavy chairs that night so we could watch a street band perform below. It was the first time I had seen and heard the street harp of Veracruz, along with the big bass guitar called the *guitarrón*. My son, who was little then, fell asleep on my lap as we counted the ships by their lights far out in the bay.

The hotel has changed some, but only a little. The town has less flowers—bougainvillea, pink oleander, and hibiscus—and certainly more cement. The market hasn't changed, though, the long *malecón* (beach promenade) is still there, and the shrimp are as good as ever.

Mazatlán is an Indian name for "place of the deer." It is an old port, but still actively exporting goods to the Far East. It has a wide, sweeping bay and a latitude that permits the most spectacular pink and blue sunsets. It also has the second highest lighthouse on the North American continent, helped a bit by being on a tall hill above the sea.

Most of the tourist action is right at seaside and sea level, although this is also a base for busy hunting and fishing activity. Mazatlán was also my introduction to the outskirts of a tropical city, and the modesty (also known as poverty) on the fringes was pretty staggering. (I had already seen the edges of the dusty desert towns.) Somehow, one becomes accustomed to this in Mexico, and I say this not as one oblivious to Third World needs, but as one who loves the country and knows its monumental shortcomings and problems.

Many of the homes on the beach front are painted in chintz—bright colors, with front patios of tile and with iron fences and gates. The hotels string along the *malecón,* culminating in a big clump on the north beach. Restaurants are scattered among the hotels but there are some good ones also back in town near the market. Everyone orders shrimp in Mazatlán, prepared in every conceivable way, in cocktails and omelets, broiled, grilled, batter-fried, sautéed, etc.

One version I liked was *Camarones Fritos a la Francesa* (French Fried Shrimp). These were batter-fried and the light crispness came from using beer. Since it was Mexico, and they don't import beer, I use Mexican beer just to be authentic. Maybe Mexican beer is the secret in beer batter. . . .

CAMARONES FRITOS A LA FRANCESA
(French Fried Shrimp)

2 pounds large shrimp
1 cup flour
¼ teaspoon salt
2 whole eggs
3 tablespoons melted butter
1 cup beer
2 egg whites, stiffly beaten
Hot lard

Shell and devein shrimp and rinse and pat dry. Mix flour with salt. In a separate bowl beat eggs lightly with butter and stir in flour mixture. Add beer slowly and stir only until batter is no longer lumpy. (Don't overstir.) Let batter ferment in a warm spot for about 45 minutes, then carefully stir in egg whites. Dip shrimp in batter and fry in hot lard (enough to cover shrimp as they are frying). Drain on paper towels and serve with small bowls of mayonnaise and *Salsa Verde* (page 79). Serves 5.

Scrambled eggs are as popular in Mexico as they are here, at least in the hotels and restaurants, but the eggs are usually scrambled with bits of ham and sometimes tomatoes. The more elaborate concoction, *Pisto,* is scrambled eggs with vegetables, ham, and the tiny *chile pequín.* It is a hearty meal when served with fresh fruit and hot *bolillos* or *pan dulce* (sweet bread).

PISTO
(Scrambled Eggs with Vegetables and Ham)

⅓ cup oil
¾ cup chopped green onions
1½ cups each diced cooked potatoes, raw zucchini, and cooked ham
1 cup fresh or frozen peas
½ teaspoon oregano
1 *chile pequín* (dried red chile), crumbled between your fingers
12 eggs, lightly beaten
Salt and pepper

Heat oil in a large frying pan and sauté onions for 2 to 3 minutes, then add potatoes and zucchini. Cook over a low-medium heat for 3 to 4 minutes and stir in ham, tomato, peas, and seasonings. Continue to cook until all ingredients are heated through. Add beaten eggs that have been lightly salted. Scramble mixture over a low-medium heat, stirring gently to keep the eggs from sticking. Salt and pepper to taste. Serves 6.

There is a very interesting vegetable that comes from Mexico and is now imported into parts of the United States. It is called *jícama,* and is tuberous-looking like a rutabaga. The skin is tough and brown but the flesh is sweet and crisp—a cross between a mild turnip and a water chestnut. Fruit and vegetable carts which are common in Mexico—big two-wheeled boxes, some with awnings—are full of slices of *jícama,* pieces of pineapple, and half-peeled mangoes on sticks, all served with a squeeze of lime and a dusting of cayenne pepper. The pepper is wonderful on the fruit, and it's amazing to see how these snacks sell to all ages and types—from street kids to business-people. Not too many men in suits reach for mangoes, but I'm impressed by how daintily Mexicans can consume something as disastrously messy as a mango. But then, after all, they are used to using a soft tortilla as a scoop or utensil.

CHAPTER TEN

The Northwest

ALAMOS

*F*ROM Mazatlán north to the United States border the scenery becomes less and less enchanting. However, I happen to be such a fan of Mexico and have entered the country so many times at the western crossings that I cannot help but have fond memories of the region. Many of my first impressions were made along this route, and some of them have never changed.

For instance, Mexico's star-crossed love affair with modern plumbing is a continual source of amusement to me. (I conquered the annoyance years ago.) The very first night I spent in a motel in Mexico, in the northern city of Hermosillo, no water would, or could, be coaxed out of the faucet of the bathroom sink. This forced me to brush my teeth in the shower, which, as if to make up for the sink, came on like gangbusters with no way to control the volume. I would say that seven out of ten experiences with Mexican plumbing have been like this first one. As I mentioned before, there is remarkable technical and engineering skill among Mexicans, but maintenance is not their forte.

Another thing I noticed when first traveling into the country was how many scraggly-looking dogs were hanging around the villages and on the outskirts of the towns. Coming from this fussy, pet-oriented country I was shocked to see these animals groveling for food and looking abused. It was a naive judgment really, in a country where the basics are scarce for many, and where people are expected to participate, as much as possible, in providing their own food. Naturally, any animal that can scavenge, and most of them can, is expected to look out for itself. In truth, Mexicans really like animals and accept them in and around their lives very easily. Naturally they think we are a little odd-acting toward our pets.

A wonderful memory of the northwest, and of the northeast too, is the introduction to Mexican beef. The great plains of northern Mexico make wonderful grazing land, and while the cattle look pretty lean compared to ours, the meat is very flavorful. But because it is so lean it also tends to be tough which accounts for the popular preparation techniques. Mexican beefsteak (*bifstek*) is sliced thin and pounded even thinner, then fried or grilled quickly. Both pork and beef are often boiled to tenderness and then shredded. Beef *filete* (fillet), the exception, is deliciously tender, and often used in *Carne Asada,* or in mimicking any American-style steak. (I really can't praise the meat enough—or the fish or fowl either for that matter). In Guanajuato, I had a beef-liver butcher and a pork-liver butcher. Both of them sliced the liver very thin and I fried it so no blood ran; it was delicious and the pork liver was especially mild.

In Culiacán, the capital of the state of Sinaloa on the western coast, we filled warm, fresh flour tortillas with *Carne de Res en Chile Colorado* (Beef in Red Chile). These *chiles* are the dried version of a chile similar to the Anaheim chile or *chile verde* which is raised and sold in the southwest of the United States.

CARNE DE RES EN CHILE COLORADO
(Beef in Red Chile)

2 pounds lean stewing beef, cut in ½-inch pieces	½ teaspoon powdered cumin
Water	½ teaspoon oregano
1 teaspoon salt	3 peeled garlic cloves
3 *chiles colorados*	Salt
1 cup water	3 tablespoons oil

Put beef in a stew pan and just barely cover with water. Sprinkle with salt and bring to a boil; then reduce heat. Cover and cook until tender (about 2 hours) and water is nearly cooked away. Core and seed chiles and place in a saucepan with water. Cover and simmer for 10 minutes, then transfer chiles and water to blender. Add cumin, oregano, and garlic and blend until smooth (should be the consistency of gravy). Salt to taste. Remove cooked meat from stew pot. Heat oil in same pot, add chile purée and cook for 3 to 4 minutes. Add meat and heat through, coating meat with purée. (Add a little water if needed.) Serve in warm, flour tortilla and/or alongside *Refritos* (page 93). Serves 4 to 5.

Culiacán's unusual name is from Nahuatl. It is a town that was built in many different locations before finally settling between the coast and the Sierra Madre Occidental mountains. The city, like Guadalajara, owes its existence to the maniacal Nuño de Guzmán, president of the First Audiencia of New Spain. This was the first ruling group after Cortés, and Guzmán has one of the blackest reputations in the history of the country, especially in this area where he exploited the Indians beyond endurance. This tyranny and intolerance finally led to his explusion, in chains, from New Spain. But Guzmán did leave the beginnings of Culiacán, a city which is now a big agricultural center, especially in the production of tomatoes. It is also the home of the *Carta Blanca* brewery—producing a good beer.

Further up the coast is Los Mochis, still in Sinaloa, and an interesting little city, most of which I have discovered quite unintentionally over the years. (I don't know why, but I always seem to have car trouble in Los Mochis and must stay there while the car is being repaired.) This is also a major farming center around which the fertile growing area is due to the advanced irrigation techniques employed and to the two large dams which regulate the water supply. Not only are cotton, rice, and vegetables grown around Los Mochis but there is a big sugar cane field with a mill that was started by an American in the early part of the century. As a result, quite a number of Americans have lived in Los Mochis over the years. Maybe this is why Los Mochis boasts of having a purified water system, making it possible to drink water from the tap. Los Mochis is also the turning point to euphoniously named Topolobampo,

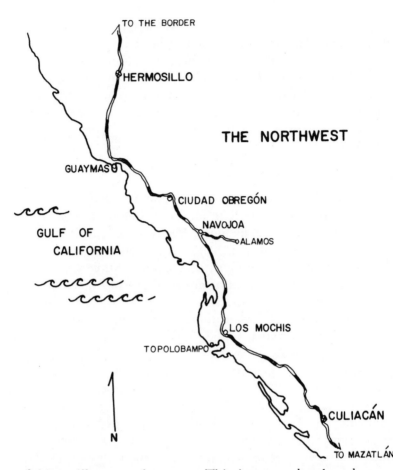

TO THE BORDER

HERMOSILLO

THE NORTHWEST

GUAYMAS

CIUDAD OBREGÓN

NAVOJOA

ALAMOS

GULF OF
CALIFORNIA

LOS MOCHIS

TOPOLOBAMPO

N

CULIACÁN

TO MAZATLÁN

a fishing village on the coast. This is not a developed resort
site, but it is a port for lots of sport fishing boats, a site for duck
hunting expeditions, and has some rather nice beaches. It's also
the end of the line for the train ride from Chihuahua city along
the famed Copper Canyon. This canyon, and there are many
in the state of Chihuahua, is said to be larger than the Grand
Canyon and is a very spectacular sight from the train. You can
take either a fast or slow train from Chihuahua city, and on my
next trip to Mexico, I'm going to take the slow one. At
Topolobampo you can take a ferry to La Paz in Baja California
to round out an interesting affair with the public transportation
system of Mexico.

Incidentally, public transportation is good in Mexico, and you have several classes from which to choose. I think the buses go down to fourth-class—those are the vehicles on which people take their farmyard with them. Because Mexican life, both rural and urban, still revolves heavily around central markets for food shopping, people come in from the *ranchos* and *barrios* each morning to buy and sell; therefore buses are important. I rather favor second-class buses, at least in the summer, because the windows open. Often, in the more modern, first-class buses the air conditioning is temperamental. If you are taking a train to anywhere that requires traveling overnight, a Pullman is much more preferable than the coach car. Mexicans are wonderfully oblivious to crying babies and it's hard to sleep on a coach train.

I remember boarding a train in Tepic years ago. The Pullman was full and I foresaw a long sleepless ride to the border in the coach car. I suggested to my son that HE ask the train official is there was a chance to get a bed for the night, knowing the Mexican kindness to children. The uniformed employee smiled and said he would try, impressed with Lee's Spanish. The night wore on and Lee fell asleep and I dozed, but there was no summons to sheets and a pillow. When we stopped in Mazatlán, the same man came and picked up my very-sound-asleep son and beckoned for me to follow. Several cars later we were given a berth in the Pullman with the man putting my son down on the bed so gently that he never awoke. I still think the best way to travel in Mexico is with a vanguard of children.

The boundary of the states of Sinaloa and Sonora comes about halfway between Los Mochis and Navojoa, a not particularly impressive town on Route 15. Another agricultural center, this time for cotton, Navojoa is also the center for the Mayo Indians. To the east, in the mountains, live the Tarahumara Indians, a still quite primitive tribe which is protected by the federal government. Although their religion reflects some early Jesuit influence, it is mostly based on ancient customs and superstitions. The Tarahumaras were considered fierce fighters in the early days and successfully held out against the Spanish.

Navojoa's major feature is that it is the turnoff to the charming, oddly-placed, colonial town of Alamos, once a wealthy silver mining town, and the capital of the area before it was divided into the states of Sonora and Sinaloa. Alamos was established in the early sixteenth century and was a stop on the El Camino Real (The King's Highway) between Mexico City and San Francisco, until revolution and mining failures reduced the town to another past and lost colonial monument. It is, in fact, a national monument now and the government has strict rules against any new building. Americans discovered Alamos in this century and part of its restoration has come from their investment. It also bears the unique distinction of being the home of the Mexican jumping bean. A certain plant that grows wild around Alamos has a bean wtih an active larva inside that jumps when warmed, making the bean dance in your hand. An enterprising Mexican discovered this curiosity and made it quite famous and himself quite wealthy.

Alamos has a couple of very nice restaurants where regional specialties are served. Hearty soups—more like stews—are called *pucharos,* and this recipe, *Sopa de la Cena,* was probably made for the tired and hungry ranchhand after a long day on the wind-swept plains of northern Mexico. *Cena* is the Spanish word for the light and late evening supper in households where the main meal, the *comida,* is eaten in the early afternoon. However, a hungry *ranchero* needs more than bread and fruit.

SOPA DE LA CENA

(Supper Soup)

2 pounds meaty (country-style) pork spareribs, cut into serving pieces
1 bay leaf
1 medium onion, thinly sliced
1 teaspoon salt
Water

3 tomatoes, peeled, cored, and chopped
1 teaspoon oregano
3 cups sweet corn
3 *chiles serranos,* stemmed and minced
Lime wedges

In a soup pot, put meat, bay leaf, onion, and salt. Cover amply with water and bring to a boil. Cover, reduce heat and simmer for 2 hours. Cool soup and skim off top fat. Add tomatoes, oregano, and corn and simmer for 30 to 45 minutes longer. Serve soup in deep bowls along with small bowls of chopped chiles and lime wedges. Serves 5 to 6.

Less than an hour north of Navojoa, on Highway 5, is the agri-industrial city of Ciudad Obregón. This modern, flat city is easy to identify because it has one of the widest main thoroughfares in Mexico, and because it is so very "uncolonial." It is, in fact, so full of cement that without trees or angles of shelter, the heat of summer can be overwhelming. But I have a fond recollection of Ciudad Obregón. On my first trip to Mexico, we stopped, a couple of streets away from the mainline of traffic, at a restaurant that looked like something out of a Pancho Villa movie. This restaurant was part of an old hotel that was crumbling, but still not without charm. The dining section, in better shape, but also old and authentic, was open for the *comida.* We ordered the special of the day, a thin but tasty beefsteak, beans, and very narrow *Enchiladas de Mole*— which are simply enchiladas filled with a small amount of *queso fresco* and dipped in a *mole* sauce. It was a memorable meal and I have been to that restaurant several times since, but not for several years, so I don't know if it is still there.

On a later visit I had a salad there and, for the first time, tasted the *nopal* cactus paddle. The paddles were cut into small pieces and tossed with onions, tomatoes, cilantro and *queso fresco*. Because the pieces of the *nopal* were small, the salad was called *Ensalada de Nopalitos.* This use of the affectionate diminutive ending (in this case *"ito"*) is common in Spanish-speaking cultures. Mexicans are always talking about their little house, child, dog, cat, visit to town, etc. This added description of tinyness carries over into descriptions of volume and length, also. One of the classic Mexican gestures is using the forefinger and thumb and trying to make the smallest possible space between them, without touching, to show how small something is or was. It's done, of course, with the appropriate accompanying facial expressions. Spanish also employs augmentative endings to describe gross exaggeration that is not complimentary and often ridiculing. These endings slow down the need for endless adjectives, and, in my opinion, give a very funny and charming touch to the language.

ENCHILADAS DE MOLE
(Enchiladas in a *Mole* Sauce)

1 recipe for *Mole Poblano con Guajolote* (page 73)
24 corn tortillas
Oil
1 pound *queso fresco* (page 96) or Farmers cheese

Sliced radishes
Shredded lettuce

Follow recipe for making *mole* but eliminate the turkey and the 8 tablespoons of lard used for browning the turkey. Keep *mole* warm in a frying pan. Soften the tortillas in a little oil which has been heated on a griddle. Dip each softened tortilla in the *mole*, sprinkle a little cheese in a strip down the middle of the tortilla, and roll. Place rolled tortillas in a shallow oven dish keeping them very close to each other to keep warm. When all tortillas are rolled, reheat *mole* sauce, pour over enchiladas, and garnish with sliced radishes and shredded lettuce. Serve with *Refritos* (page 93). Serves 8.

ENSALADA DE NOPALITOS
(Nopal Salad)

4 cups raw *nopal* cactus pieces

½ small onion, thinly sliced

1 large tomato, cored and diced	2 tablespoons olive oil
¼ cup chopped fresh cilantro	2 tablespoons red wine vinegar
1 teaspoon oregano	Salt and pepper
½ cup crumbled *queso fresco* (page 96) or Farmers cheese	
1 *chile serrano*, stemmed and minced	

Rinse and drain *nopal* pieces and mix with onion, tomato, cilantro, oregano, cheese, and chile. Chill for 1 hour. Just before serving toss with oil, vinegar, and salt and pepper to taste. Serve on lettuce leaves. Serves 4 to 5.

Guaymas is the only seaside stop on the main highway north. Physically the city is quite pretty with a fine natural harbor that is backed by high mountains. It is a popular sports fishing spot for people from the southwestern United States since the Sea of Cortés (the Gulf of California) is abundant with all types of fish and shellfish. It's an active commercial harbor, too, and vast quantities of shrimp and oysters are shipped from here to the United States.

The town buildings are worthy of some sightseeing since the community was established early in Mexican history as a base for the energetic mission Fathers, Kino and Salvatierra. But, like many Mexican seaports, Guaymas has also had its military and pirate invasions during the last hundred years, and it endured a lot of conflict during the Mexican revolution of this century. Now, however, it is a busy tourist stop with a pleasant coastal climate and lots of nighttime activity. I've had all kinds of fish dishes in Guaymas, but on this last trip I had oysters baked in the shell with a characteristic Mexican sauce poured over them—just the taste I like.

OSTIONES DE GUAYMAS

(Guaymas Oysters)

28 to 32 medium-sized oysters
⅓ cup olive oil
1 small onion, minced
3 cloves garlic, minced

¼ cup lime juice
2 dried *chile pequín*, crushed
Salt and pepper

Open oysters and reserve liquid. Discard top shell. Heat oil in a frying pan, add onion and garlic and sauté over a low heat until softened. Remove from heat and add oyster liquid, lime juice, and crushed chiles. Add salt and pepper to taste. Spoon mixture over each oyster and place oysters in a pan under a broiler, about 3 inches from flame or coil. Remove when edges of oyster just begin to curl. Serves 4.

Hermosillo is the last major stop before crossing the border back into the United States. It's a genuine city, the capital of the state of Sonora, housing the state government and the University of Sonora. The city is clean with wide, shaded streets, an oasis of sorts as the area around is really desert. Hermosillo serves as an overnight stop for many travelers, going north and south or as the turnoff to sports fishing facilities at Kino Bay, seventy miles west on the Gulf of California.

Tortillas de Harina (Wheat Flour Tortillas) are common in the northern part of Mexico, especially in Chihuahua and Sonora, and there is a deep-fried *burrito* (pork or beef stuffed in wheat flour tortillas) that also can be found in this region of the country. In Hermosillo, the latter is a specialty of one little restaurant. These *burritos* have a way of growing on you so that a stop in Hermosillo would not be complete without a *chimichanga*. Sometimes they are called *chivichangas*.

TORTILLAS DE HARINA
(Wheat Flour Tortillas)

Scant 4 cups wheat flour

1½ teaspoons salt
½ cup lard
1 scant cup water

Mix flour with salt and cut in lard. Then stir in water with a fork. (Dough will be sticky.) Knead dough until smooth on a floured surface, then return to bowl and let sit covered for 1½ hours. Divide dough into 16 to 18 balls about 2 inches in diameter. On a floured surface, roll out each ball with a well-floured rolling pin until very thin, using a circular motion to make the circle even. Cook on a hot griddle or frying pan for about ½ minute on each side. (Blisters will appear, break and turn brown.) Repeat this process with all dough balls. Serve warm. Makes about 16 to 18 8-inch tortillas.

CHIMICHANGAS
(Deep-Fried Meat *Burritos*)

1 large onion, finely chopped
3 cloves garlic, mashed
3 tablespoons oil or lard
2 cups cooked pinto beans (*Frijoles,* page 93)
2 *chiles jalapeños,* stemmed, seeded, and minced
2 cups cooked ground beef or cooked

shredded beef (page 16) or cooked shredded pork (page 79)
½ teaspoon cumin
1 tablespoon vinegar
Salt
16 wheat flour tortillas
Oil or lard
Guacamole (page 157)
Crema (page 119) or sour cream

In a frying pan, sauté onion and garlic in oil or lard until softened. Drain beans, reserving liquid, and add to frying pan.

Mash beans with onions and garlic, adding liquid as necessary to make a slightly moist mixture. Continue to heat adding chiles, meat, cumin, and vinegar and salt to taste. When mixture is hot, put about 2 tablespoons in the middle of a tortilla, fold like an envelope, and secure with a toothpick. Fry stuffed tortillas in 1 inch of hot (375°) oil or lard until browned on both sides. Drain on paper towels and serve hot with *guacamole* and *crema* or sour cream. Makes 16.

NOTE: These can be made ahead and reheated in foil in a 350° oven (12 to 15 minutes from the refrigerator, and 25 minutes from the freezer).

From Hermosillo the drive to the border crossings is long and uneventful—nothing but flat desert with rocks and cactus and a few small settlements. It's a real winddown from the heart and life of the country, and even though the transition out of Mexico is slow, I still feel an immediate change when I enter the United States. Again, it's not the language or the architecture, or superficial distinctions such as uniforms or flags. And no matter how eager I am to get back to my friends and family and the familiarity of my own country, I start to miss Mexico almost immediately.

WEIGHTS AND MEASURES

THE METRIC SYSTEM

In the Metric System the *meter* is the fundamental unit of length, the *liter* is the fundamental unit of volume, and the *kilogram* is the fundamental unit of weight. The following prefixes, when combined with the basic unit names, provide the multiples and submultiples in the Metric System.

milli . . . . one thousandth (.001)
centi . . . . one hundredth (.01)
deci . . . . one tenth (.1)
deca . . . . ten (10)
hecto . . . . one hundred (100)
kilo . . . . one thousand (1,000)

WEIGHT CONVERSION (Mass)

U.S. Customary Units		Metric Equivalents	
Ounces (oz.)	Pounds (lb.)	Grams (g.)	Kilograms (kg.)
½	1/32	14.175	.014
1	1/16	28.35	.028
4	¼	113.40	.113
8	½	226.80	.227
12	¾	340.20	.340
16	1	453.60	.454

1 kilogram (1,000 grams) equals 2.2 pounds

VOLUME CONVERSIONS (Capacity)

| U.S. Customary Units | | | | | | Metric Equivalents | |
Tea-spoons (tsp.)	Table-spoons (tbsp.)	Fluid Ounces (fl. oz.)	Cups (c.)	Pints (pt.)	Quarts (qt.)	Deci-liters (dl.)	Liters (l.)
1	1/3	1/6	1/48			.05	.005
3	1	1/2	1/16			.15	.015
6	2	1	1/8	1/16		.30	.030
12	4	2	1/4	1/8		.60	.060
24	8	4	1/2	1/4	1/8	1.20	.120
36	12	6	3/4	3/8	3/16	1.80	.180
48	16	8	1	1/2	1/4	2.40	.240
				1	1/2	4.80	.480
				2	1	9.60	.960

Fractions of a cup in thirds are not shown in this table.

NOTE: Do not confuse the present British System with the Metric System. British countries use the same system of weights as in the United States, but their cooking utensils (cups and spoons) are slightly larger than those used in the United States and Canada. British countries, also, are now converting to the Metric System.

TEMPERATURE CONVERSIONS

Fahrenheit and Celsius (often known as Centigrade) temperatures may be converted into each other by using the following simple equation:

$$\text{Fahrenheit} = 9/5 \text{ Celsius} + 32°$$

$$\text{Celsius} = 5/9 \text{ (Fahrenheit} - 32°)$$

Fahrenheit	Celsius	Fahrenheit	Celsius	Fahrenheit	Celsius
−40	−40	149	65	329	165
−31	−35	150	65.5	338	170
−22	−30	158	70	347	175
−13	−25	167	75	350	176.6
− 4	−20	176	80	356	180
0	−17.7	185	85	365	185
5	−15	194	90	374	190
14	−10	200	93.3	383	195
23	− 5	203	95	392	200
32*	0*	212	100	400	204.4
41	5	221	105	401	205
50	10	230	110	410	210
59	15	239	115	419	215
68	20	248	120	428	220
72	22.2	250	121.1	437	225
77	25	257	125	446	230
86	30	266	130	450	231.1
95	35	275	135	455	235
100	37.7	284	140	464	240
104	40	293	145	473	245
113	45	300	148.9	482	250
122	50	302	150	491	255
131	55	311	155	500	260
140	60	320	160	600	315.5

As you may have noticed, oven ranges (Fahrenheit scale) begin at 150° (or warm) and increase by 25° to 550° or 600° (or broil). Celsius gauges will probably be numbered from 65° to 315°.

*Water freezes at these temperatures.

INDEX

Carta Blanca brewery, 185
Casa de las Artesanías de Jalisco,
    122, 123
Casas, Las, 103
Casas, Bartolomé de las, 102
Castillo, El, 51
Castillo de San Diego, El, 155
Celaya, 145
Cena, 188
Cerro de las Campanas, El, 146
Ceviche (Raw, Marinated Fish), 160
Chafing Dish Dam, 117
Chapala, 120
Chayotes Rellenos (Stuffed
    Chayotes), 124
Cheese:
    broiling, 14
    fresh, 189
    with fried tortilla chips, 14
    stuffed, 55
Chetumal, 47
Chiapas, 99, 100, 103, 104
Chiapas de Corzo, 100
Chichén-Itzá, 51, 52, 60
Chichén, New, 51
Chicken:
    in a banana leaf, 57
    drunken, 83
    enchiladas, 68
    in onions, 70
    soup, 18
    strips of, 139
Chihuahua, 10, 186, 192
Chilaquiles (Tortilla Hash), 173
Chiles:
    Anaheim, 32, 184
    California, 32
    green, 32, 184
    jalapeño, 39
    pequín, 178
    poblano, 33
    rellenos, 32
    strips of, 31
    tuna stuffed, 32
Chili(es) (*see* Chiles)
Chimichangas (Deep-Fried Meat
    Burritos), 193
China poblana, dress, 72
Chivichangas, 193

Chocolate:
    caliente (hot chocolate), 112
    history of, 3
    hot, 112
Cholula, 77
Chongos (Rennet Custard), 110
Chorizo, 85
Chorizo de Toluca (Toluca Pork
    Sausage), 85
Cilantro, pungency of, 2
City Dump (disco), 52
Ciudad, 162
Ciudad Obregón, 189
Cobá, 49, 50
Coco Loco, 172
Coctél Campechana Marinera
    (Campeche Shrimp and Oyster
    Cocktail), 61
Coctél Presidente (President's
    Cocktail), 51
Coffee (*see* Beverages)
Colima, 162
College of San Nicholas Obispo,
    111
Comida, 188, 189
Comotes de Santa Clara (Sweet
    Potatoes of Santa Clara), 74
Compostela, 173
Consomé de Pollo (*see Sopa de Pollo*)
Copper Canyon, 186
Cora Indians, 174
Córdoba, 68, 69
Cortés, 37
Cozumel, 50
Crema (Mexican Soured Cream),
    119
Cuautla, 80, 81
Cuernavaca, 77, 78, 80, 82
Culiacán, 184, 185
Custard (*see* Desserts)

Degollado Theater, 122
Desserts:
    Almond, 75
    banana:
        in eggnog, 101
        fried, 37
    candy, Celaya caramel, 145